The Collected Poems, 1957-2004
Robert Sward

For Amy + Scott —
in Friendship
Trust we'll see you
again soon!

The Collected Poems, 1957-2004

Robert Sward

8.14.04

Santa Cruz

Black Moss Press
2004

National Library of Canada Cataloguing in Publication

Sward, Robert, 1933-
    The collected poems of Robert Sward, 1957-2004.

ISBN 0-88753-392-2

    I. Title.

PS8587.W35A17 2004   C811'.54   C2004-901865-5

Author photo by Paul Schraub
Cover by David Alpaugh

Published by Black Moss Press at 2450 Byng Road, Windsor, Ontario
N8W 3E8. Black Moss books are distributed by Firefly Books, 66 Leek
Crescent, Richmond Hill, ON Canada L4B 1H1. U.S. orders should be
directed to Firefly Books at 4 Daybreak Lane, Westport, CT U.S.A. 06880-
2157.

Black Moss gratefully acknowledges the generous support given by the
Canada Council for the Arts and the Ontario Arts Council for its publishing
program.

ONTARIO ARTS COUNCIL
CONSEIL DES ARTS DE L'ONTARIO

Le Conseil des Arts | The Canada Council
du Canada | for the Arts

Gloria in Excelsis

My children and grandchildren: Cheryl, Kamala, Michael, Hannah, Nicholas - Aaron, Robin, Maxine and Heron

* * *

With thanks to Elissa Alford, Heidi Alford, Jonathan Alford, David Alpaugh, Charles Atkinson, Ellen Bass, Rose Black, Robert Bly, Dr. Rachel Callaghan, Maria Elena Caballero-Robb, Ruth Daigon, Dion Farquhar, Jack Foley, Dana Gioia, Heidi Alford Jones, Peter Gilford, James D. Houston, Dr. Ed Jackson, Coeleen Kiebert, Patrick McCarthy, Mort Marcus, Doug McClellan, Bruce Meyer, William Minor, Neil Roberts, Tilly Shaw, David Swanger and Hannah Sward.

My thanks, too, to Marty Gervais and Black Moss Press for their generosity and commitment to my work.

* * *

"...All things counter, original, spare, strange;
Whatever is fickle, freckled (who knows how?)
With swift, slow; sweet, sour; adazzle, dim;
He fathers-forth whose beauty is past change:
Praise him."

—Gerard Manley Hopkins, "Pied Beauty"

* * *

"Five mysteries hold the keys to the unseen: the act of love, and the birth of a baby, and the contemplation of great art, and being in the presence of death or disaster, and hearing the human voice lifted in song. These are occasions when the bolts of the universe fly open and we are given a glimpse of what is hidden; an eff of the ineffable. Glory bursts upon us in such hours: the dark glory of earthquakes, the slippery wonder of new life, the radiance of ... singing."

—Salman Rushdie, "The Ground Beneath Her Feet"

ALSO BY ROBERT SWARD

POETRY
Advertisements, Odyssey Chapbook Number One, 1958
Uncle Dog & Other Poems, 1962
Kissing The Dancer & Other Poems, Introduction by William Meredith, 1964
Thousand-Year-Old Fiancée, 1965
Horgbortom Stringbottom, I Am Yours, You Are History, 1970
Hannah's Cartoon, 1970
Quorum/Noah (With Mike Doyle), 1970
Gift, 1971
Five Iowa Poems, 1975
Cheers For Muktananda, 1976
Honey Bear On Lasqueti Island, B.C., 1978
Six Poems, 1980
Twelve Poems, 1982
Movies: Left To Right, 1983
Half-A-Life's History, Poems New & Selected, Introduction by Earle Birney, 1983
The Three Roberts, Premiere Performance, 1984
(Featuring Robert Priest, Robert Zend and Robert Sward)
The Three Roberts On Love, 1985
The Three Roberts On Childhood, 1985
Poet Santa Cruz, Introduction by Morton Marcus, 1985
Four Incarnations, New & Selected Poems, 1991
Rosicrucian in the Basement, Introduction by William Minor, 2001
Three Dogs and a Parrot, 2001
Heavenly Sex, New & Selected Poems, 2002

FICTION
The Jurassic Shales, A Novel, 1975
Family, with contributions by David Swanger, Charles Atkinson, Tilly Shaw, 1994
A Much-Married Man, A Novel, 1996

NON-FICTION
The Toronto Islands, An Illustrated History, 1983
Autobiography, Contemporary Authors, Volume 206, 2003

EDITED BY ROBERT SWARD
Vancouver Island Poems, An Anthology, 1973
Emily Carr: The Untold Story, 1978

AUDIO CDs
Rosicrucian in the Basement, as read by the author. (Recorded for the KPFA-FM
    Program "Cover to Cover," Berkeley, CA), 2002
Robert Sward: Poetry, Review & Interview with Jack Foley (Recorded for the
    KPFA-FM Program "Cover to Cover," Berkeley, CA), 2002
Writers' Friendship, Jack Foley and Robert Sward (Recorded for the KPFA-FM
    Program "Cover to Cover," Berkeley, CA), 2003

CONTENTS

UNCLE DOG BECOMES A BODHISATTVA:
AN INTRODUCTION TO ROBERT SWARD'S
COLLECTED POEMS

You don't look like a Canadian.

—Saul Bellow to Robert Sward

*   *   *

All I am really hungry for is everything.

—Robert Sward

Reminiscences from Cornell University, forty years ago: I remember the eyes most of all: large, hazel-brown, luminous, kindly. And the manner: hesitant but pleasant. And the sense one had of a gentle, oddly elegant madness. He was tall: one thought he must look like Robert Lowell. And there was insight: he would stammer, but there were always ideas, intelligence, something worth listening to. And the oddity of the poems:

> I did not want to be old Mr.
> Garbage man, but uncle dog
> who rode sitting beside him.
>
> Uncle dog had always looked
> to me to be truck-strong
> wise-eyed, a cur-like Ford
>
> Of a dog. I did not want
> to be Mr. Garbage man because
> all he had was cans to do.

("Uncle Dog: The Poet At 9")

Robert Sward's career began in the late 1950s. He is a well-known poet, but he is not nearly as well-known as he should be. Sward's poems are often comic, but they are never *only* comic—or for that matter *only* seriocomic. X.J. Kennedy is a seriocomic poet of considerable capacity, but he is nothing like Sward who actually has more in common with W.B. Yeats, for whom the Trembling of the Veil of the Temple was a constant source of inspiration. Sward's poems are the result of a plunge into a never fully ironized, often hilarious sense of mysticism: they are the product of a rest-

13

less, spiritually adventuresome sensibility masking itself as a stand-up comedian. Who but a mystic would write a passage like this—funny, but alive with the *via negativa*:

> The dodo is two feet high, and laughs.
> A parrot, swan-sized, pig- scale-legged
> bird. Neither parrot, nor pig—nor swan.
> Its beak is the beak of a parrot,
> a bare-cheeked, wholly beaked and speechless
> parrot. A bird incapable of
> anything—but laughter. And silence:
> a silence that is laughter—and fact.
> And a denial of fact (and bird).
> It is a sort of turkey, only
> not a turkey, not anything. —Not
> able to sing, not able to dance
> not able to fly.

("Dodo")

Sward describes himself as "Born on the Jewish North Side of Chicago, *bar mitzvahed,* sailor, amnesiac, university professor (Cornell, Iowa, Connecticut College), newspaper editor, food reviewer, father of five children, husband to four [now five] wives[1]...."

Sward's mother died in 1948 at the age of 42; her last words were a request "to keep [Robert's] feet on the ground." The poet describes his podiatrist father as handsome—"a cross between Charlie Chaplin and Errol Flynn"—as well as "ambitious and hard-working," a "workaholic." By the time Sward wrote the poems collected in *Rosicrucian in the Basement,* the father has blossomed into a full-fledged eccentric, a visionary adrift in a world which doesn't comprehend him:

> "There are two worlds," he says lighting incense, "the seen
> and the unseen...
> This is my treasure," he says.

Like uncle dog, Sward's father is a comic version of the poet—but the terms have changed a little. Sward's father quotes Rilke (albeit unknowingly):

> "We of the here-and-now, pay our respects
> to the invisible.
> Your soul is a soul," he says, turning to me,

---

1 Contemporary Authors, A Bio-Bibliographical Guide, Volume 206, Gale/Thomson, 2003

"but body is a soul, too. As the poet says,
'we are the bees of the golden hive of the invisible.'"
"What poet, Dad?"
"The poet! Goddammit, the poet," he yells.

("Rosicrucian in the Basement")

It was only after his mother's death that the father became interested in Rosicrucianism and the world of the "invisible." Sward points out that the year his father became "a strict and devout" Rosicrucian was also the year that he, Robert, flunked algebra. The father's later amorous adventures with "Lenore" (shades of Poe) give the son the wonderful poem, "Lenore and the Leopard Dog." "I've told you before, dear," says the father, "God rewards you for kissing."

Like his father, Sward "lives in another world." But the young man is not so certain which world that is. When his father says, "As above, so below"—the famous formula attributed to Hermes Trismegistus—the son answers, "I'm not so sure." The word "below" is partly ironic since the podiatrist father is always talking about feet—"God has feet like anyone else. You know it and I know it"—and because the father carries out his rituals in the basement. Yet it is also a serious assertion about the relationship between the world of the senses and the "other" world. Sward's own impulses led him away from both Rosicrucianism and his family's Judaism to the East. In "Prayer for My Mother," one of his most moving and accomplished poems, Sward is accused of being a "Jew who got away," a "sinner." But he also celebrates one of his meditation teachers, Swami Muktananda, "the biggest party animal of them all":

> Seven years I hung out with him,
> even flew to India, meditated
>   in his cave
> chanting to
>   scorpions, malaria mosquitoes
> so illumined they chanted back.

("The Biggest Party Animal Of Them All")

Sward writes, "I... was nicknamed 'Banjo Eyes,' after the singer Eddie Cantor. Friends joked about my name: "The Sward is mightier than the Sword." And because I had a zany imagination, I had only to say, "Hey, I have an idea," and other eight-year-olds would collapse laughing. I was regarded as an oddball, an outsider. I had few friends.

15

Robert Sward learned early that the comic, the "zany," was a mask by which one could assert oneself—through which one would be listened to. In his poems, the mask remains, but it is at the service of an essentially visionary impulse: "the vision, the life that it requires." The word "dream" haunts his work. Sward remains simultaneously "not so sure" and utterly certain:

> For two, maybe three, minutes
> I saw two worlds interpenetrating
>
> jewels into jewels,
> silver suns, electric whiteness,
>
> World 'A' and world 'B'
> one vibrating blue pearl,
>
> world like a skyful of blue suns
> Whoosh! Whoosh! Whoosh!
> ("The Biggest Party Animal Of Them All")

Neither in "this world" nor "the other," Chicago-born, a U.S. Navy veteran who served a stint in the combat zone in Korea (1952), Sward moved to Canada in 1969 to take up a position as Poet-in-Residence at the University of Victoria. While there he began to practice yoga, started a publishing company (Soft Press), met and for twelve years was married to a Canadian. Indeed, two of his children are Canadian citizens as is Sward himself—in truth, a citizen, at heart, of both countries. At once a Canadian and American poet, one with a foot in both worlds, Sward also inhabits an enormous in-between. It will come as no surprise to readers to find that his poems get at the moment of truth by being deeply unsettled, by refusing to rest in any particular other than the cosmic ambiguity of the wholly visionary and the wholly sensual. Past, present and future—and their tenses—assail him equally:

> As a teacher, I talk. That's present.
> For thirty years as a teacher, I talked. That's past.
>
> It may only be part time, but I will talk. That's future.
> ("Turning 60")

"During the late 1960s and early '70s," the poet writes, "American men arriving in Canada were automatically assumed to be Vietnam War protestors, draft dodgers, or deserters... in 1969, I was a married, thirty-six-year-old, honorably discharged and decorated Korean War veteran. I was also the father of three children." Again the oddball, the outsider.

Sward taught at the University of Victoria from 1969 to 1973 and worked in Toronto from 1979 to 1985, when he returned to the United States.

In January 1986, Sward moved from the mountains overlooking Monterey Bay (California) to Santa Cruz, a seismically active community of forty-five thousand people located seventy-five miles south of San Francisco. Another milestone.

Sward's friend, poet Morton Marcus remarked that "the physical and psychical environment [took] him by the tongue to new spiritual heights, which... slowed his responses to a meditative stillness and (surprisingly) eased him back into such closed forms as sonnets and villanelles." In Santa Cruz, while earning a living as a freelance journalist, Sward served as food reviewer ("Mr. Taste Test") and, on one occasion, as the world's skinniest Santa Claus.

Sward's multiple marriages were by no means a source of pride: "I find each divorce hurts hurts hurts just as much, maybe more, than the one before... I have come to agree with Robert Graves, who says the act of love is a metaphor of spiritual togetherness, and if you perform the act of love with someone who means little to you, you're giving away something that belongs to the person you do love or might love. The act of love belongs to two people in the way that secrets are shared... Promiscuity seems forbidden to poets..."

In June, 1987 Sward met visual artist Gloria Alford, also originally from Chicago. Sixteen years later Robert and Gloria are still together, and thriving.

Robert Sward's poetry has undergone many shifts—including, as Marcus points out, the shift to closed forms—but its fundamental impulse seems not to have changed since I first came upon it in the early 60s. Outwardly "zany" and fanciful, it is inwardly serious, troubled and questioning. He has written over twenty books of poetry as well as some fiction and non-fiction; in the late 1980s he entered the Internet, poems a-flying. He has produced CDs. He once described himself as "a heat-seeking cocky mocky poetry missile... a low-down, self-involved dirty dog. Woof woof." He has noted how many of his poems have "to do with love, divorce, multiple marriage, aging, loss, and the challenge of bringing up children in a highly unstable world." He identifies strongly with strange and sometimes hostile animals.

What is sought in all this work is liberation, illumination—*it*.

The joy of his writing is the joy of the quest. "The only thing better than being employed," he says, "is being unemployed." He has recently turned 70 and is producing work as fine as what he was producing forty years ago. He has not grown up exactly, but he has grown. "These days," he says, "I'm paying more attention to Ben Franklin ['Early to bed, early to rise, makes a man healthy, wealthy and wise.'] and less to Blake with his lines about "the road of excess". 'From beyond the grave the poet's father counsels him, "Spend some time at the Invisible College."

When Robert Sward was a child his Rosicrucian father asked him, "So, Bobby, you too want to see God?" There is wisdom in Robert Sward's poetry, but it is the kind of wisdom we call "crazy." The final "message" of this work is not to transcend intense contradiction (or "doubleness," as he would say) but to live deeply, even joyously, within it:

> I hardly unpack
> and get ready for this lifetime and it's time
>
> To move on to the next...

("Mr. Amnesia")

—Jack Foley, Berkeley/Oakland, CA

AUTHOR'S NOTE:

Ram Dass says, "Old age is about harvesting whatever your life's work has been." At seventy I don't feel especially old, but my life's work has been, and continues to be, poetry and, fifty years after my first publication, this is harvest time. From the thousand or so poems I've written since the early 1950s, these are the ones I'd like to preserve. Because it draws on some earlier collections, *Half A Life's History: New & Selected, 1957-1983; Four Incarnations, New & Selected, 1957-1991;* and *Heavenly Sex, New & Selected* (among others), I have come to think of this volume as something of a 'Collected Selected.' However, I have included a few newer poems like "Life Is Its Own Afterlife," for example, to round off a sequence of poems for my father.

With respect to the recent narratives, the "Father" poems, I'd like to encourage readers of the opening sections of *Rosicrucian in the Basement* and *Heavenly Sex* to begin with the title poem of the first book and "Son of the Commandment" (in *Heavenly Sex*), and read straight through to "God's Podiatrist" in the first instance and to "Life Is Its Own Afterlife" in the second.

Uncle Dog, 1962

UNCLE DOG: THE POET AT 9

I did not want to be old Mr.
Garbage man, but uncle dog
who rode sitting beside him.

Uncle dog had always looked
to me to be truck-strong
wise-eyed, a cur-like Ford

Of a dog. I did not want
to be Mr. Garbage man because
all he had was cans to do.

Uncle dog sat there me-beside-him
emptying nothing. Barely even
looking from garbage side to side:

Like rich people in the backseats
of chauffeur-cars, only shaggy
in an unwagging tall-scrawny way.

Uncle dog belonged any just where
he sat, but old Mr. Garbage man
had to stop at every single can.

I thought. I did not want to be Mr.
Everybody calls them that first.
A dog is said, *Dog!* Or by name.

I would rather be called Rover
than Mr. And sit like a tough
smart mongrel beside a garbage man.

Uncle dog always went to places
unconcerned, without no hurry.
Independent like some leashless

Toot. Honorable among scavenger
can-picking dogs. And with a bitch
at every other can. And meat:

His for the barking. Oh, I wanted
to be uncle dog—sharp, high fox-
eared, cur-Ford truck-faced

With his pick of the bones.
A doing, truckman's dog
and not a simple child-dog

Nor friend to man, but an uncle
traveling, and to himself—
and a bitch at every second can.

THE KITE

I still heard Auntie Blue
after she did not want to come down
again. She was skypaper, way up
too high to pull down. The wind
liked her a lot, and she was lots of noise
and sky on the end of the string.
And the string jumped hard all of a sudden,
and the sky never even breathed,
but was like it always was, slow and close
far-away blue, like poor dead Uncle Blue.

Auntie Blue was gone, and I could not
think of her face. And the string fell down
slowly for a long time. I was afraid to pull it
down. Auntie Blue was in the sky,
just like God. It was not my birthday
anymore, and everybody knew, and dug
a hole, and put a stone on it
next to Uncle Blue's stone, and he died
before I was even born. And it was too bad
it was so hard to pull her down; and flowers.

WHAT IT WAS

What it was, was this: the stars
had died for the night,
       and shone;
and God, God also shone,
up, straight up, at the very
top of the sky.

        The street
was one of the better suburbs
of the night, and was a leaf,
or the color of one in the
moonlit dark.
        She, my mother,
went to the window. It was
as late as night could be
to her.
        She looked at the wind,
still, the wind,
          ...never having blown.

And in the morning, now, of sleep
the stars, the moon and God
        began
once more, away,
        into the sky.

—And she, my mother, slept...
in her window, in her sky.

A WALK IN THE SCENERY

It is there. And we are there. In it.
Walking in it, talking, holding hands.
The nickel postcard—the glossy trees;
the waterfalls, the unsuspecting
deer. A scene shot from a car window:
a slowly moving car, with many
windows, and a good camera.
And we are walking in it. We tell

ourselves, quietly, perhaps screaming,
...quietly, "We are walking in it."
And our voices sound, somehow, as if
we were behind windows, or within.
We embrace, and are in love. The deer
we are watching, at the same time
(through cameras, binoculars, eyes...)
so perfectly wild, and concerned
—with the scene they are, their glossy fate
silence, Nature, their rotogravure pose—
that they remain, not watching; rather,
staring away from us, into the
earnest, green and inoffensive trees.

DODO

The dodo is two feet high, and laughs.
A parrot, swan-sized, pig-, scale-legged
bird. Neither parrot, nor pig—nor swan.
Its beak is the beak of a parrot,
a bare-cheeked, wholly beaked and speechless
parrot. A bird incapable of
anything—but laughter. And silence:
a silence that is laughter—and fact.
And a denial of fact (and bird).
It is a sort of turkey, only
not a turkey; not anything. —Not
able to sing, not able to dance
not able to fly...
          —The Dutch called it the 'nauseous bird,'
Walguögel, 'the uncookable.'
Its existence (extinct as it is)
is from the Portuguese: *Duodo,* 'dumb,'
'stupid,' 'silly.' And the story of its
having been eaten on Rodrigues
Island by hogs, certain sailors & monkeys:
Didus ineptus. A bird that aided
its own digestion, of seeds and leaves,
by swallowing large stones. It has been called,
though with birds (extinct or otherwise)
crosses are a lie, a cross between

a turkey and a pigeon. The first,
it is claimed, won out; and, having won,
took flight from flight (its wings but tails, gray
yellow tufted white). And for reasons
as yet unknown.

           Its beak is laughter
and shines, in indifference—and size.
It has the meaning, for some, of wings:
wings that have become a face: embodied
in a beak... and half the dodo's head...
It laughs—silence, its mind, extends from its ears:
its laugh, from wings, like wrists, to bill, to ears.

HELLO POEM

Hello wife, hello world, hello God,
I love you. Hello certain monsters,
ghosts, office buildings, I love you. Dog,
dog-dogs, cat, cat-cats, I love you.
Hello Things-In-Themselves, Things Not Quite
In Themselves (but trying), I love you.
River-rivers, flower-flowers, clouds
and sky;
        the Trolley Museum in Maine
(with real trolleys); airplanes taking
off; airplanes not taking off; airplanes
landing,
        I love you.

The IRT,
BMT; the London subway
(yes, yes, pedants, the Underground)
system; the Moscow subway system,
all subway systems except the
Chicago subway system. Ah yes,
I love you, the Chicago El-
evated. Sexual intercourse,
hello, hello.

      Love, I love you; Death,
I love you;

      and some other things, as well,
I love you. Like what? Walt Whitman,
Wagner, Henry Miller;
      a really
extraordinary, one-legged
Tijuana whore; I love you, loved
you.
      The *Reader's Digest* (their splendid,
monthly vocabulary tests), *Life*
and *Look*...
      handball, volleyball, tennis;
croquet, basketball, football, Sixty-
nine;
      draft beer for a nickel; women
who will lend you money, women
who will not;
      women, pregnant women;
women who I am making pregnant;
women who I am not making pregnant.
Women. Trees, goldfish, silverfish,
coral fish, coral;
      I love you, I
love you.

Kissing The Dancer, 1964

KISSING THE DANCER

Song is not singing,
          the snow

Dance is dancing,
          my love

On my knees, with voice
          I kiss her knees

And dance; my words are song,
          for her

I dance; I give up my words,
          learn wings instead

We fly like trees
          when they fly

To the moon. There, there are
          some now

The clouds opening, as you, as we
          are there

                    Come in!

I love you, kiss your knees
                    with words,

Enter you, your eyes
          your lips, like

                    Lover
Of us all,

          words sweet words
          learn wings instead.

MARRIAGE

I lie down in darkness beside her,
this earth in a wedding gown.
      Who, what
she is, I do not know,
nor is it a question the night
would ask. I have listened—

      The woman
beside me breathes. I kiss that,
a breath or so of her, and glow.
      Glow.
Hush now, my shadow, let us...

Day breaks—

      depart.
Yes, and so we have.

LOST UMBRELLAS

She enters a room exuding displeasure,
      strewing bits of string, grievances,
      bottle caps,
            hairnets,
      law books,
      like largess
to all corners.

From the seams of her change purse
      leak
      Travelers Cheques,
photos of used-car salesmen
      (dear brothers-in-law),
strychnine,
      ragged old horoscopes
and gifts of broken glass.

Daughter to the planet Saturn,
mother to my wife—

Her courtiers, we direct her,
mix martinis for her
find causes for her, lost umbrellas
        and car keys
even at the gates of hell.

BY THE SWIMMING

By the swimming
the sand was wetter
the farther down you dug; I dug:
my head and ear on top
of the sand, my hand felt water...
and the lake was blue not watching.
The water was just waiting there
in the sand, like a private lake.
And no one could kick sand
into my digging, and the water
kept going through my fingers slow
like the sand, and the sand was water too.
And then the wind was blowing everyplace,
and the sand smelled like the lake,
only wetter. It was raining then.
Everybody was making waxpaper noises,
and sandwiches, kicking sand
and running with newspapers on their heads.
Baldmen and bathing hat-ladies, and naked people.
And all the sand turned brown and stuck together
hard. And the sky was lightning, and the sun
looked down sometimes to see how dark it was
and to make sure the moon wasn't there.
And then we were running: and everybody was under
the hotdog tent eating things, spitting very mad
and waiting for the sky, and to go home.

CHICAGO'S WALDHEIM CEMETERY

We are in Chicago's Waldheim Cemetery.
I am walking with my father.
My nose, my eyes,
        left pink wrinkled oversize
        ear
my whole face is in my armpit.

We are at the stone beneath which lies
my father's mother.
There is embedded in it a pearl-shaped portrait.
I do not know this woman.
      I never saw her.
I am suddenly enraged, indignant.
I clench my fists. I would like to strike her.
My father weeps.
He is Russian. He weeps with
      conviction, sincerity, enthusiasm.
I am attentive.
I stand there listening beside him.
After a while, a little bored,
      but moved,
I decide myself to make the effort.
I have paid strict attention.
I have listened carefully.
Now, I too will attempt tears.
      They are like song.
      They are like flight.
I fail.

"...I HAVE JUST BOUGHT A HOUSE"

DEAR GEORGE—George, I have just bought a house,
an eighty-seven room house. Also,
a twenty-one room house. And many
little houses. And eighteen trailers,
and nineteen cars (six with beds in them);
and wives for all the rooms, the trailers
the little houses, and the six cars
with beds in them,
      ...and they all love me,
all my wives love me. They do, George. They
write to me. Every day. They write
to me. And they are perfect, concise
and beautiful letters. They say—
Yes, and they say it eighty-seven times.
And then sign their names. I taught them how,
           George,
myself. How to read and write. How to—

in houses. How to love, and how to
write perfect, concise and beautiful
letters. Yes, and how never to die.
How to live forever, for me, for
me, even though I will die. And how
to make me feel as if I won't, even
though I will, will feel as if I will.
And they are very good at it.
        Anyway,
they are all pregnant, George,
           all my wives
are pregnant. Even the parakeets.
Because some of them are parakeets.
And some are goldfish,
           silverfish, ants
rats, goats, skunks...
       and all have borne me children,
parakeet, silverfish, ant, rat
       goldfish
children.
       And I'm happy, George. I like
marriage, really like it. Wives,
        bedbugs
and getting mail every day.
And I feel I have a place to go.
It feels good.
       The only trouble is
I don't have any money, or even
any silverfish or rats or bed sheets
a newspaper, or a place to go.
I mean, why don't I, George?
       I live alone
in an old upright typewriter,
      with but
one dog and two cats to work
to cook, to drink beer with me.
It's sad, George. We cry ourselves
to sleep. We are so alone.
Now and then Dog sings to us—

Woof, woof.
Pale cats, pale man
you shall have houses,
you shall have wives;
night falls

Woof, woof.
Beer for you, milk for you,
sleep for you, dreams for you.
Sleep my children,
sleep my children,
sleep. *Woof, woof.*

It is a lovely song, George,
and Dog sings it well.
        We sleep.

        Witches,
nightmares big as houses, wives
warts, mushrooms,
            they are all there is.
Night-things. Things—
            pressing all the keys
around us. Wanting what? To kill us,
to put us into jail.

        Dog,
Dog barks, he barks songs at them.
They type Death onto his back,
onto his tail, his ears, his tongue.
            Fleas and lice!
We dance to avoid
the keys. We do not dance well.
We are typed into dreams, into wives.
Into mansions and swans.
            Old bed sheets, Death-sheets,
                    bedbugs
            pushcarts and poems.

SCENES FROM A TEXT

Several actual, potentially and/or really traumatic
situations are depicted on these pages.
—Transient Personality Reactions to Acute or
Special Stress (Chapter 5).

Photo II

The house is burning. The furniture
is scattered on the lawn (tables, chairs
TV, refrigerator). Momma—
there is a small, superimposed white
arrow pointing at her—is busy
tearing out her eyes. The mute husband
(named, arrowed) stands idly by, his hands
upon his hips, eyes already out.
The smoke blankets the sky. And the scene,
apart from Momma, Poppa, the flames...
could be an auction. Friends, relatives
neighbors, all stand by, reaching, fighting
for the mirrors, TV, sunglasses;
the children, the cats and speechless dogs.

EMU: A LECTURE FOR VOICES; FOR STEREO

Three-toed, one-headed, its wings the size
of chicken-feet—and largest (next to
the ostrich) of all existing birds...
the emu stands, colossal, ratite
six feet high
         its god enplumaged, dark
hidden in the dismal, drooping, soft
brown hair.
         Its hips, hump, its bulge, perhaps
of flightlessness, or sky—appear as speed;
the stunted cause, the befeathered, round
sloping, still embodiment of speed.

The emu runs, swoop-skims, a two-shanked
one-humped, egg-hatched camel: the bird most
like a camel.

Avoiding deserts
however, the emu inhabits
open fields and forests where, keeping
in small companies, it feeds on fruit
(of the emu tree), herbage and roots...
now and then booming, with subsequent,
and peculiarly hurried efforts,
at breeding.
Extinct, in Tasmania
on Kangaroo, King and Wing Islands,
the bird is found, and in small numbers,
in Southeastern Australia.

IT BREEDS
Its nest, as if it had been rolled in
and humped (in reverse), is a shallow
sandy, green-egg-filled pit, the eggs of which, all
nine (to thirteen), are incubated
by the cock, an earnest, familial
type of ostrich.

The young, at birth, bear thin
length-striped down, are wattleless, and walk;
cursed, crane-necked, blank, dull adult-eyed
baby, camel, ostrich-ducks...
in file
swift, point-beaked,

mothered, three-toed, one-headed
—an image, but for the stripes (and down),
of itself, in age.
Its booming note, god
and size, are at rest in it, in its
conspicuous state of egglessness.
It screams, booms, bounds

...BECOMES IMMENSE, FLIES
extinct, shaggy, stripe less (in age)

FLOATS
its head in the camel clouds, the hump
the bulge, the sandlessness that is God.

ATTIC BY THE RIVER

I walk by the used river
each day
        past an old attic
(no house, the attic only
beech trees growing through it)
in a field. The river smells
of barges, rotting timbers
        waterskiers' boats, lovers
the very sun upon it.
Rivers age in Connecticut,
grow feeble, irritable
and complain like old women.
The charred attic, too,
        complains
bears ill-will toward people,
        weeps
and cries, and talks aloud
on certain evenings
        to the sea.

MOTHERS-IN-LAW

Married twice now, I've had two
mothers-in-law. One visited us
and required, upon departure,
the services of three gentlemen
        with shoehorns
to get her back into her large black
Studebaker.

        The other, Momma-law the Present,
is (with the exclusion neither
        of that other,
        my wives
        nor the fathers-in-law
        of either marriage),
that Studebaker.

NIGHTGOWN, WIFE'S GOWN

Where do people go when they go to sleep?
I envy them. I want to go there too.
I am outside of them, married to them.
Nightgown, wife's gown, women that you look at,
beside them—I knock on their shoulder blades
ask to be let in. It is forbidden.
But you're my wife, I say. There is no reply.
Arms around her, I caress her wings.

SOCRATES AT THE SYMPOSIUM

Sonnet For Two Voices

Of Love, my friends (after such sophistry
and praise as yours), may one presume? Well, then,
let me begin by begging Agathon:
Good sir, is not your love a love for me?
And not a love for those who disagree?
Yes, true! And what is it that Love, again,
is the love of? Speak! *It is the love again
of "Socrates."* Love then, and the Good, are me.

Explain! Is Love the love of something, or
the love of nothing? *Something!* Very true.
And Love desires the thing it loves. *Right.*
Is it, then, really me whom you adore?
Or is it nothing? *O Socrates, it's you!*
Then I am Good, and I am yours. *Agreed!*

BARBECUE

—*For William Dickey*

I

They were spraying Pepsi and moth-juice
on the fire. The mosquitoes, lawn flies
and moths dove, flashed and were painlessly
consumed. There was applause

          ...we entered.

And while my wife was kissed, they clapped
me on the back. They wanted to know
that I was there. And then I kissed them
down their throats, choked and knew that they were there.

And after I had kissed those who had
kissed my wife, and after they kissed me,
we sprayed one another, scratched and dove
after the moths. We flashed, painlessly,
and emerged to munch the ashes, coals
to sip moth juice, lemon juice and gin.
And (again) we clapped one another
laughed, kissed, sipped, puffed and swallowed cigarettes.

II

The cat-girl would not believe in it
and crouched there pained, purring with the pups;
(their tails were remarkably alike
and neither pronounced upon events
with them.) From time to time they'd lick one
another, or the cream dip, but otherwise
were still
           ...though one of the pups had tried
the fire, and the cat-girl
           sleekly swallowed gin.

III

Someone found Lil, the wife of no one,
buried beside the spit. She wanted
a martini; we obliged, and then
reburied her.

Bernie dove in after the moths
only to be buried, topped, beside the spit.

IV

The sky was rainbow strips of chrome, clouds
and the sun, the great, archetypal

Ford: pork-sauced and on the suburban
spit of heaven.
        And Lil's angel waved
free, fulfilled and married now, to chrome
...sipping gin and tonic.
                We all stared,
climbed upon our spit, and then dove
in after the moths.
            —The fire attained to Lil.

The fire was a Ford, without chrome, pure
as gin, as cream dip, moths or spray, death
and we sang to it: its attaining
to heaven, to Lil, to space, ourselves
and the archetypal Ford.

In the other distance, in the space
the consuming that is east, the night
beyond where the moths take form, beyond
what we flash for when we die,
                we sense
the white-walled dawn, time and tomorrow's
Ford.
        There was Mars,
the suburban star of barbecue.

V

The party had somehow failed. The cards—
and there was Rummy, large as Lil, four'd
the evening star. It was time for gin
and time for light!
            No one would admit
that he was there; we hid in front of
one another's wife. The women hid
beside the flames, the way they flickered
through their eyes. I kept trying to put my tongue

into their cards, into their eyes, ears
throats, between their teeth; but theirs were there

between mine. I bit them. And they cried
with half their tongues
                    munching diamonds and spades.

And the bushes had begun the moon,
ending "gin," martinis and marriage.

Suddenly the women screamed. The moon
burst through, revealing their husbands, the pup-girl

themselves. The bushes became the lawn;
the night, the earth; and the moths, the sun.

The men became their wives; and the wives
became the men, for the most part

re-marrying themselves. The men were asleep
beside their wives, smiling, spitted, still

illicit. —Morning. My wife and I
sipped gin. I was Bernie, and she the moths.

CHICAGO

There are many underground things
in cities, things like sewers,
that run for miles, lengths
and widths, across cities,
under all. Then there are
the basements of large stores,
houses and hotels, and often
these basements run for twenty feet
and more out, around the buildings;
and coal, garbage and all kinds
of food are sent up and down into
the basements, or out, from the side-
walks and the alleys and streets,
by chutes, corrugated elevator-
stands, iron platforms, sewer tops
...round, rectangular or square.

And these metal things in the sidewalks,
streets, are always rather warm;
and in the winter, to comfort
and unbitter their sittings,
haunches and tails, and to avoid
the asphalt ice and cold, cats
and dogs, stray squirrels
and so forth, come at night
and from miles around, rest
and together partake.

        And from some
distances, they and their live optic
green, brown congregations of eyes
appear as islands, still yellow
large, oval, gray or opalesque.

And no dog bites no cat, nor squirrel,
and all is quiet, idle, until the sun
comes up and chases them
out of the night, off the warmth
and good of the sewers to their parts
and tails. Then without a look
at the sun, itself, they run, trot
walking, no, no business into the snow.

ALL FOR A DAY

All day I have written words.
My subject has been that: Words.
And I am wrong. And the words.
    I burn
three pages of them. Words.
And the moon, moonlight, that too
I burn. A poem remains.
But in the words, in the words,
in the fire that is now words.
I eat the words that remain,
and am eaten. By nothing,
by all that I have not made.

Thousand-Year-Old Fiancée
& Other Poems, 1965

MOVIES: LEFT TO RIGHT

The action runs left to right,
cavalry, the waterskiers—
then a 5-hour film, *The Sleeper,*
a man sleeping for five hours
(in fifteen sequences),
sleeping left to right, left to right
cavalry, a love scene, elephants.
Also the world goes left to right,
the moon and all the stars, sex too
and newspapers, catastrophe.

In bed, my wives are to my left.
I embrace them moving left to right.
I have lived my life that way,
growing older, moving eastward—
the speedometer, the bank balance
architecture, good music.
All that is most real moves left to right,
declares my friend the scenarist,
puffing on a white cigar, eating
The Herald Tribune, the *New Republic.*

My life is a vision, a mechanism
that runs from left to right. I have lived badly.
Waterskier, I was until recently
in the U.S. Cavalry. Following that
I played elephant to a lead by Tarzan.
Later, I appeared in a film called *The Sleeper.*
Till today, standing on the edge of things,
falling and about to fall asking, Why?
I look back. Nowhere. Meanwhile, one or more wives
goes on stilts for the mail.

ARRIVAL

The light goes out, the dark comes down,
small cries, low murmurs of foxes.
A light descends on the trees, whitish like what
they themselves give off. Watching it, I am moved

to prayer, to the crying out of titles
of certain poems, the names of God,
my own name. It takes shape before me.
It is the night's name, my wife's name.
In motion, in one another's arms,
we arrive somewhere where none of this is so.

AT JIM McCONKEY'S FARM

All is quiet and we lie here numbed.
There is motion, rough-winged barn swallows
and clouds. Butterflies loop around one another
suggesting bows, configurations of a knot.
Both of us lose interest. The corrugated
galvanized roof of a 100-year-old barn
refuses light. The sun comes off it
in unexpected intensities. The fields and hills
form a backdrop to this. Cicadas and song sparrows.
The landscape rolls, my eyes roll with it.
Uneasily at first, unexpectedly it comes over me
that no one will ever not love here.
The new clothespins, the look of light on the line.
Old barns. Orchards. The John Deere harvester.
I am overwhelmed by the complexities
of skunk cabbage.

　　　　It is warmish. The breeze pleases me.
Everything is dry. We stand and walk
around in the day. We walk out to the barn
with the corrugated top. Hours later we drink beer
and ponder the hollows under stars.
I have no thoughts whatsoever. I glance at her
and embrace her, but have nothing to say.
Implausible phrases, song titles, clichés—
　　　　they come haltingly to mind.
Then the few convictions I have done well by.
We hold hands and walk around there.
No debts. No debts. Twelve years of manuscripts.
We can go in or out. At this moment,
for this day even, we have belonged here.
How did it happen? What have we affirmed?
We kiss the one star's lips. And always, married still
　　　　we move on.

HOLDING HANDS

Always I am leaving people, missing them,
going out to them and loving them;
holding hands, doing turnabout, ah,
going to movies with them, clowning
reverential, an enthusiast—for what?
The certain good of sleeping with them,
holding them, climbing into their bellies.
I am present in them, approving their skins,
most foolish hopes, warmest impulses
            and the loss
of vanity, the presence of which—
and all is lost.

            Huge stars are falling,
great owls circle above us. We sit here
in wonderment—

            Is there anyone
anyone anyone has not been with?
The truth is, nothing else matters.
You are, I am, he is. The world will please
come to order. Be seated. Hold hands.
No it won't. No it won't. Don't be scared.
Cover up my love, we will all of us
never not be in you, my love love's there first.

THOUSAND-YEAR-OLD FIANCÉE

We are alone, Death's thousand-year-old fiancée
and I. The thing suggests itself to me.
I step onto the front parts of her feet,
and stand like that facing her saying nothing.
In moments I lose twenty pounds and sweat. My nose
            bleeds.
It occurs to me I may never before
have acted out of instinct. We do not embrace.
She is in her middle sixties, with varicose veins,
whitish hair and buttocks as large as Russia.
Things come off of her in waves, merriment,

exuberance, benevolent body lice,
hundred-year-old blackheads. I kiss her hives.
I lick her nose that shows she drinks bottles
and bottles of vodka every day.
I am standing there in my Jewish hair
facing her with my life. Knock, knock.
It is Death in spats and a blue business suit.
I stand there in my Jewish hair facing him.
He is very still, grinning, grayish, bemused.
Pretty soon I begin to scream. All night I scream.

Yeah. After a while I go under and kiss
her ass. It takes a bit. Fathers and sons,
I am up to my knees in the moon.
Kiss this ghost she says of a certain light.
I plunge my tongue into it to the ears. Madam,
I say, astounded, choking, feverish,
I have not as yet had you. Have me, she says.
Under my foreskin there is a star, whole
constellations. Goddammit, I am not
speaking to you here of sex! Kiss me here,
she says. Kiss me there. Stars, ghosts and sons,
                    winged,
we are all of us winged—
                    the one thing
there is of us. Death, you old lecher,
I affirm you, I confront you with my balls.
I revere dead fish and sunken submarines,
the little red schoolhouse and the American way.
Let us in fact join hands with the universe.
Death, I have news for you. I climb into
your young fiancée eleven times a night.
There are signs that she is pregnant.
Death, there is nothing I will not love.

PEOPLE COMING OUT OF PEOPLE

Rings coming out of rings,
          four and then eight—
you reach for one, the man says,
and you have two. That is the way

rings give birth to rings. Once speaking of cups
he cried, Each is within the other,
each is linked to each. All that he did
bore witness to this. "You are pop art,"
said his woman. Marriage is like that.
What is virtue? Reach for one
and you have two. Weariness,
that is also a truth. All conditions
are truths. Claim only those
you've a mind to. All things, all truths are gifts.
The man who dreamt of playing magician
reaching for goblets, chalices, cups
one and then within it its mate,
or linked by the handles, by rims,
like women within women
the metaphysics of sex.
That too is a question—
the man reaching,
            all that he wants, doubles.
That is the way rings give birth to rings
and that is what if not a truth? (again)
cups within cups, people within people
out of love, out of need, out of want.

HALSTED ST., CHICAGO

It is Chicago, it is Chicago
I am trying to plug in,
my finger in my navel, in Halsted Street
with holes in it; an electric light socket,
            buzz, buzz—
I want very badly to plug in.
I put my left forefinger in my ear,
and my other forefinger, I put that
exactly on the nose
            between the eyes
of Little Orphan Annie, who appears daily
            (twice daily, in fact)
on the back pages
of the *Chicago Tribune*.

I can't stand holes. I kiss people when they talk,
or put my finger in.
Also railroad tracks. I walk on them.
One day it rained. I walked for fourteen hours.
I walked all the way north to Wisconsin.
And it is true, it was good to learn:
If people see that you care for them
they do not mind your plugging in.
Coming home, no one on the bus minded
        my plugging in.
I plugged in to their buttonholes
        and shoes
        (the shoelace eyes in them).
I came back strong,
I came back with all my fingers
        and my toes too,
back once and for all now.

I unscrewed the telephone. I put my fingers in.
Click, click, the operator.
I stammered out my message, my latest coming,
deepest feelings, vibrations, revelations...

A failure to understand me.
Anger on my part. And a new urge to plug in.
The bent coin release, the holes in urinals,
God's left eye, heaven too, outer space
the ionosphere, the stratosphere
        the Milky Way
        and Universe in general.

CHICAGO PUBLIC LIBRARY

I am downtown. I am wearing sunglasses,
        phony nose,
and big inch-and-a-half-long
        false teeth.
I have them jammed on over
my other teeth.
I have the look of unabashed stupidity.
People comment on it.

Some hoodlums jeer at me,
        throw rocks at me.

It is raining. Also, it is snowing.
There are carols. It is December,
        late December,
nearly Christmas.

Old men and women are huddled in the corridor
of the Chicago Public Library.
I go there and huddle too.
I keep on my sunglasses and nose.
People like them. They admire them.
Then they look at me. They look closely,
and huddle against me. They pick my pockets,
        my pubescent blackheads,
my father's watch chain.
One of them, a dwarf, takes me by the hand.
We go walking, just the two of us.
After a while, we begin to fly.
We fly very slowly and low
and toward the Lake. And then back.

I fall asleep. I have bad dreams;
I awaken—

Waldheim Jewish Cemetery,
the Outer Drive,
stainless steel florist shops,
the traffic lights,
red, amber and green.

I enter off Montrose Avenue.
Slowly, slowly
I begin the long swim
        to Michigan.

SATIRES

THE NEW YORK TIMES BOOK REVIEW

This critic in bed with this poet,
in bed with this female writer
of scenarios,
O General X., O General Y.,
beneath the bed,
but in it nonetheless,
Dr. Spock,
Dr. Edward Teller, proud father
of the H-Bomb, I see you there...
you are there too, reviewed by RAND,
planting mushrooms in the chamber pot.

O Dr. Strontium, O Folk Medicine
encyclopedias of saleable wars,
picture books of extinct everything,
aphrodisiacs, erotica—

Historians embracing historians,
novelists embracing novelists,
their hands on one another's crotches,
pens in one another's pockets;
books
in one another's books.

O hold me,
hold me close, I want to sleep there too,
where the warmth is, where the money is,
aura
of martinis. Reserve a bit of sheet
for me, I want in, I want in
with the New English Translation
of the Bible, Writers' Workshop teachers
O and all the others of America's
O charming, honey-fingered men of letters.

AMERICAN HERITAGE

This, O my stomach, is a painting
of the Civil War. Look—Antietam.
All over there are dead,
noble Northern, noble Southern, dead.
One, no, no, several, wear beards.
They are all General Ulysses S. Grant beards,
noble, truly noble beards.
The Union side, O my soul, see them!
All, all of them waving,
resembling, bearing the name
Walt Whitman. They are all on horseback,
all with maps and swords, banners
and copies of last Sunday's
New York *Times* Book Review
watching through binoculars,
writing letters, keeping journals,
reading *Leaves of Grass*...

And there is Barbara Frietchie.
Hi, Barbara. Barbara's pregnant.
She is soon to be the mother
of Abraham Lincoln, Dr. Oliver Wendell Holmes
and Carl Sandburg.

This is an historical moment,
very historical. You can feel it
and read about it, too
(and General Stonewall Jackson,
Clare Booth Luce, Robert E. Lee
      and many others),
in *American Heritage,*
edited by Bruce Catton,
with whose kind permission
I herewith reprint this painting.

     *   *   *

Song: *There's No War Like Civil War*

O the Civil War's
the only war,

the only war, the only war;
the finest war,
yes, the noblest most unforeign war,
the finest only noblest most
unforeign war
that ever I did see. (Chorus, etc.)

SUDS IN TERRYCLOTH—MR. & MRS.

Ahh, froths she, her soap chip teeth
to Mr. Terry S.

She like he is in her "clean clear through"
(and deodored, too!) bathrobe.

Raising her FAB right arm, one hand
against the armpit

And the other at her wrist, he gnaws
and drools into the terrycloth.

Ahh, cries she, her teeth and tongue
at him. She seems pleased.

He grins and glistens from his eyes.
He licks her then, up

And down her spine, Ahh!
licked-lipped, she runs her tongue…

"Dazzling white (to be sure), but
something more. It's as if

"Suds and sunlight had combined
to Terry swiftly, agilely through

"And up and down her robe. No wonder he
can't keep his tongue away!"

Ahh! Its thick, soft white nap
outdates all dulling soap scum cleanliness.

Nor is his robe without its attractions.
She sniffs his bushy belt. He reddens,

Froths into the air, and slaps
his little webbed feet hard upon the floor.

She spreads her robe to him; and he, his
to her. She moistens him

And he, her. Bursting from within their pelts,
teeth bubbles suds, ahh—

"THE VERY AIR HE BREATHES"

She lies upon a tawny mat
of effluence—and leopard spots.

And he *(he's hers
and she knows it!)*

Can but barely be seen, crouched
and to the left of her.

One ear, an eyebrow, and a bit of cheek
are all that show of him.

The caption (again) suggests that it is fun
(fabulous fun) being female

At a time like this!
And, indeed, it looks like fun.

Her eyes are huge and subtly closed
as leopard spots; and her lips are spread.

She is, in fact, a deodored leopardess
about to take the male.

But again, the caption: *You are the very air
he breathes* (the male is hard upon her).

She appears to be undisturbed by this;
and with both shaved armpits bared, she arches

For him. One is inclined to think of her
as being altogether without fear; she smiles,

And takes the male. Neither deodorant,
nor effluence, could do more.

                She smiles,
and she lies there, the very air
he breathed.

NINE-AND-A-HALF TIMES

They had killed Momma's brother Johnny
nine-and-a-half times in the war. There
wasn't hardly anything left when
he got home: of Johnny or of Momma.
I mean he came home without his arms,
without his ears, without his brains, or
hair; without his loving everyone,
                and women
that made Momma mad. He didn't like
love no more, or Momma, and he had
been married in between all the times
he was killed. Nine-and-a-half times!
And Momma had cried and cried and said
it was like his being killed. The Army
and President Roosevelt, General
Eisenhower...
                They were all sorry,
and Momma ate the letters and the envelopes;
the telegrams, and then Johnny; the Purple
Heart, the White Heart, the gold
star, Daddy & all of Johnny's wives.
And Momma was all that there was left.

REPORT FROM THE FRONT

All over newspapers have stopped appearing,
and combatants everywhere are returning home.
No one knows what is happening.
The generals are on long distance with the President,
a former feature writer for the New York *Times*.
No one knows even who has died, or how,
or who won last night, anything.
Those in attendance on them may,
for all we know, still be there.

All over newspapers have stopped appearing.
Words once more, more than ever,
have begun to matter. And people are writing
poetry. Opposing regiments, declares a friend,
are refusing evacuation, are engaged instead
in sonnet sequences; though they understand, he says,
the futility of iambics in the modern world.
That they are concerned with the history and meaning
of prosody. That they persist in their exercises
with great humility and reverence.

Horgbortom Stringbottom, I Am Yours, You Are History, 1970

IN MEXICO

San Miguel de Allende

Mail from the States,
Traffic citations,
Invitations to protest,
Revocations of credit cards,
Circulars for an improved
Prostate gland;
The John Birch Society's
Declarations
Of support: the war
In Vietnam,
The Dominican Republic.

Jabon del tio Nacho,
Soap for blackheads;
And the movies,
Cine Angela Peralta,
Hoy Jueves 17 de Junio
Lancha Torpedera 109,
Y Ricardo Corazon de Leon.

> *Under new censorship rules, no individual casualty*
> *figures were reported by military authorities. From*
> *now on terms like 'light' or 'heavy' will be used.*
> —News Item.

"Not only sad," my friend writes me, "Creepy."

(Then) It is such a destructive welcome—
Wanting to please, succeed, and living in dire fear...
I wrote a book, rewrote a novella,
Both lying around in revision.
I've been sick (physically) this year:
What a waste New York is, I've come to think.

Outpourings, hatred, disgusts.
Praise for the indecent,
Indifference
For what has moved her.

Your letters rankle,
I love them,
They are like newspapers, I say.
They set my teeth on edge.

We correspond,
Send love notes, X-rays, news clippings,
Copies of the Congressional Record.

*　　*　　*

Queretaro

I am on a bench
in the Jardin
reading Newsweek.

On my left
is Martha Washington.
On my right,
Barbara Frietchie
with a megaphone,
TV set
transistorized earrings.
I breathe into her ear,
hold her left breast.
We are tuned in
to a meeting
of Washington Republicans.
They are reading
our futures
in the entrails of snails.

Their leaders speak
with Southern accents,
faces like Rhesus monkeys,
eyes like chopped mushrooms,
voices like a lead canary.

"America," says Barbara Frietchie,
"Why are they beating on you?
How is it you smell
more and more
like a used car lot?

Auras

There are auras, there is light,
      like halos,
on all your roads.
They are standing there.
I converse with them.
"Auras," I say, "I too have died, and renew,
haunt highways, hover over trailer trucks,
high like their drivers on dexamyls.
I walk in and out of their dreams, nightmares,
      fantasies;
their mothers, their fathers;
their first, second and third wives,
dissolving, then reappearing..."

I am Death,
your Mother,
the Little Red Schoolhouse,
the nickel-plated children.
I am the little boy you made it with,
for the first time.
The barefoot prodigy.
I am your First Grade Teacher,
I am the Rabbi who taught you Hebrew,
the bank robber,
the kid who broke your jaw,
the Model-T Ford,
a Chevrolet, a Pontiac, a Chrysler,
the rumble seat,
airplanes crashing in air,
ships colliding,
      moving off into the distance.

        * * *

Gone blind,

I see
only things,

man
on a rooftop

World
one way, then another,
then another.

*   *   *

Sun slanting through clouds,
circling
the sky circling
left to right

> *Opening*
> *arches*
> *opening, the sun*
> *white rain*
> *falling*

> *·The light*
> *drifting*
> *through trees.*

*   *   *

I am dreaming you,
Why not, someone has to.
Be yourself.
Unambitious, half asleep—
I do not dream,
Or even sleep well.
Inconsistency
Is my one grace.

I know nothing.
I am the Original
Mediocre mind.
I am your son,
Yeshiva bacher;

Did I not study in my country's literature?
Minor in its philosophy?

I see your future,
I see mine.
Again,
Again. It is the world happening,
The world
With its balls,
Balls, America!

I want to live.
It is given,
The world is given.
I have come to collect my dreams.
I want my dreams. I want them now!
To declare my love,
Make an assessment,
Take inventory,
Seek directions,
Honor and attend you.

DREAMS

—For John Wayne

Everything costs.   The Revolution, featuring dreams,
                          the quality of light in Aspen, Colorado,
                          the visit here recently of John Wayne.

I woke this morning and was scratching.
Have I become an apologist for some quaint aesthetic?
How is it seven years ago, when I was first advised
        of Insurrection,
my thoughts were all of metre and the New Criticism?
At heart, I tell myself, I am an arsonist.
Yet last evening in the firehouse I was reading aloud
and then later at Guido's playing tapes
of Ronald Reagan reading Homer.

Senator Hickenlooper, I will buy you an apocalypse.
Do you want a red apocalypse, or a green apocalypse?
Would you like it seasoned with marijuana
or oregano?

All night in the mountains old men with chainsaws
are cutting their way to the moon.

Senator, let us order an investigation.
That the sun has risen.
Seven times in one day.
I am on a ski lift on my way to the moon.
Hand-in-hand with the moon,
the astronauts with chainsaws,
fire chief in my arms,
I am scratching and falling.
All my poems are burning.
And the cities are burning.
There are learned gentlemen making inventories.
There are others on their knees sucking them off.
Everyone is occupied.
I am feeling depressed,
      idle,
        a little stupid.

What will be, the unimaginable
it turns out
is only what we have been waiting for,
dinosaurs minotaurs eating the moon's genitals,
the sun in revolt,
          starting over.

          *   *   *

The light
The rain

Rocks know what the rocks say
Fire speaking with the wind

Three times the light and then the light, the Sky changes

What is it flows past stars?
Birds not flying but hopping over trees.
The writing. On pomegranates.
The word *snail,* the word for rain   wizard
butterfly

Word   for the first time.
Lovers as they read. Hair wrist neck as he tastes
her ears. Rock light the water stars

I walk downhill on my hands
the wind rising,
                    the hulls of ships
        which way
which way to the Revolution?

Five Iowa Poems, 1975

IOWA CITY, IOWA

Some years the ground pulls harder.

There are creatures in trees
whose names I do not know.
There are others in procession before us.
Pigs the size of buffalo. Cattle
the tails and markings of horses.

Iowa. What am I doing in Iowa?
Ann lies in the sun. Dozing. Depressed.
Stripping, rising on my hind legs,
hairy, cloven-footed,
Centaur, I declare myself: Centaur.
Then chicken. Then horse. Bull. Then pig.
She too: Centaur. Then chicken. Horse. Bull. Then pig.

Let us plant our dreams.
Write them down and plant them.
Plant sugar cubes.
Make love.
Then dig it up, turn it over
and plant the ground,
that ground we made love on.
What will grow there?
Rhubarb.
A peach tree.
The ground holds me as I make love to it.
How is it birds no longer fly?
Horses only. The entire state of Iowa.
I am busy planting my brains.
I will harvest them remind me please before leaving.
The time has come.
O look Centaur   Snowing   Your eyes
your eyes
they touch me.
I have been asleep.

Does it hurt?

IOWA

What a strange happiness.
Sixty poets have gone off drunken, weeping into the hills,
I among them.
There is no one of us who is not a fool.
What is to be found there?
What is the point in this?
Someone scrawls six lines and says them.
What a strange happiness.

IOWA WRITERS' WORKSHOP—1958

—For Paul Engle

Seated, against the room, against the walls
legs extended, or under chairs
iambs, trochees & knees...
we surrender, each of us, to the sheets
at hand. The author swallows his voice. Still

"Page two." Page one is saved for the last.
"The poet has here been impressed
by the relationship
between blue birds and black. In the octet
we note the crow. And its iambic death."

"On page three, *The Poet Upon His Wife,*
(by his wife) we note the symbols
for the poet: the bird
in flight, the collapsing crow, the blue bird...
Note too the resemblance between sonnets."

We vote and stare at one another's crow.
Ours is an age of light. Our crows
reflect the age, Eisenhower-Nixon
colored stripes, rainbow-solids, blacks & whites.
Ruffling their wings, Mezey, Coulette, Levine
              refuse to vote.

"Page four, *Apologies to William S.*
apologies, our third sonnet..."
And those who teach, who write
and teach, the man at hand, apologize
for themselves, and themselves at hand.

"Poets buy their socks at Brooks & Warren,
like DuPont, like Edsel, like Ike."
Anecdotes, whispers, cliques
whispering, then aloud into prominence.
Brooks & Warren, DuPont, Edsel & Ike.

Order is resumed. *"We have been here, now
forever. From the beginning
of verse."* One has written
nothing, and it is inconceivable
that one would, or will ever write again.

A class has ended. They pass by, gazing
in. The poets gaze out, and grin.
They gaze out, and through the
electric voice, the ruffled sonnet sheets
that stare against the faces staring in.

"Page one." Walled-in glances at the author.
And then the author disappears,
the poem anonymous.
Voice. Voices. There are voices about it:
anonymous. The self. A sonnet's self...

The room is filled with it. It is a bird.
It sits beside us and extends
its wings. Mezey hits it with his elbow.
The bird shrieks and sprawls
upon the floor. We surrender

We surrender to its death. The poem breathes,
becomes its author and departs.
We all depart. And watch
the green walls take our seats. Apologies.
Brooks & Warren. DuPont. Edsel & Ford.

IMPOSSIBLE HURRICANE LOSS-OF-NAME POEM

The fields planted.
Tractors   Wooden clothespins rising.
Parched. Brown. Plows and houses. Rising.
Rainbow. It ends or begins or starts.
Is it walking or is it skipping?
It rides above the fence.
If I dig a hole will I find a poem?
A pot of unicorns?
A herd of leprechauns?
I ask. The rainbow has already moved.
Seven miles in the soft light.
A field filled with cows.
The hurricane approaches.
There are funnels filled with butterflies.
Dust that is the rain.
Thunder. Trees. The grass.
The wind walking.
Phosphorous. The rain.
The noiseless. Wind. Explodes.
I am lying in the sun only there is none.
I am being blown away only
the moon rises   which
is the sun? Evening. There is none.
Red. Parched brown. Plows and houses.
Hurricane. Hurricane.
My name has been blown away.
O name poor name,
will the rain care for you as I have cared for you?
Will the wind devour you,
knock your head against a tree?
Already I have forgotten.
Can a young man named...
live happily in a hurricane?

Will his house and woman and poems blow away?
Once they have blown away. Twice. Already.
That the house and the woman and the unnamed man
have their tongues in one another's mouths,
can they go on like that?
Funnel, stars, butterfly,
wind. The noiseless
Yes, they can.

Honey Bear on Lasqueti Island, B.C.
1978

HONEY BEAR

She is a Russian honey bear
with very strong soft brown arms.
Hugging her is at once a feat
of strength, and an act of gentle surrender.

One cannot hug the honey bear
with only half a heart. It's all
or no honey bear. There's a snap
and vibrancy to her kisses

Pucker and snap—audible
across a field of wild black
berries. Honey bear loves fresh cream
and wild berries of all kinds

French cheeses and home baked bread.
She is earth tremors in the garden,
laughter in the flower beds
rough brown honey bear pulling weeds.

Her feet, large, perfectly
            proportioned
            are powerful as
angel wings. A pale blue light
surrounds her toes as she waltzes

By the clover and the mint.
Lighter than air, heavier
than a bear. Clear-skinned lady
O fairest of the fair

I bow to my honey bear.

BEAR MOTHER

            Mystery.
Familiarity. Moving together
of bodies. The dance of mouths,
hands, bellies and tongues lightly touching
            knees and hairs and milky toes.

Black bear mother with magic eyes
and dancing feet
crouching, squatting
giving birth
dropping a single cub
the cub grunting, sticky,
moaning.

BEAR MOTHER IN THE KALEIDOSCOPE

Her lips are kindly and full.
Her eyes are blue,
mouth like pale cherries
      ripe on trees
      with snow.

She appears without clothes
      or fur
in a white velvet tent
on an enchanted island.
She's a white hummingbird
at the float house
in the evening
circling clockwise
round the fire.

      *   *   *

Dark goes into light.
Dark is a black cord on a silver needle
drawn by a bear
through a cave
      shining
      glistening
in the dripping darkness
reflecting fire.

      *   *   *

In our boat at night—
with herself as passenger—
we navigate
      over rocks,

submerged, undiscovered islands,
moons like gigantic human eyes,
lunar gardens and small mansions,
wooden houses
        floating
        in the sea.

GULL, CLAM—WHAM

Gull flies up in the air
with a clam
drops it on the rocks
crack, bam, wham goes the clam

And, as it doesn't open,
gull flies up with it again.
And again drops it
        on the rocks
plop, bop, and wham again.

This time the clam opens and the gull
feasts. Gull flies up the channel
from west to east,
then back again down the same channel.

Hot summer's day.
Sun coming down.
A little breeze, out on the rocks
crack, bam, wham
        goes the clam

While we in our float house
lean out, looking to the east
and the mud flats filled with clams.
Walking out with shovels, digging
        for clams.

Gulls to the east of us
gulls to the west
gulls, gulls, clam bam wham
gulls, gulls, wham bam clam.

FLOAT HOUSE COOKING—WRITTEN WHILE SLOSHED ON LASQUETI ISLAND, B.C.

—For Maureen & Jerry Curle

Standing up to the knees
in water, he squeezes
a little lemon onto
the vegetables being sauteed

In butter on a wok
as he stands in water
in front of a Coleman stove
resting on a rock.

The rice is steaming
and the tea is brewing
the oysters are stewing
and about cooking like this
      there is no fooling

Around, silly as it may be
standing in up to the knees
pressing the garlic, opening
      the teas
being knocked over by the tide,

The main hazard of cooking
on a float house. O friends,
forgive the cook if, eating
and enjoying this dish, you feel

A little seasick or uneasy
queasy in the tummy.
Be assured, dear hungry friends,
it is not my cooking

And it is no blow to my pride
to freely admit the saltiness
of the rice is owing
      to its falling into the sea
because of the tide, you see—
not me.

Movies: Left To Right, 1983

BLIND POET

—For Marcie

She has braces on her teeth and wears
a blue and orange plaid cotton shirt:

One of fourteen students

Wiggles, chatters, finds her way
into her friends' poems.

Straightens her back like a pianist
readying herself for a performance.

Sitting upright, intent
she completes, aloud,
ahead of the others

Their own, half-formed images. "Dammit, Marcie,
whose poem is this?"

They squirm, they squabble, and defer.
Composing herself,
both hands moving smoothly

Over an embossed, a Braille keyboard
of otherwise blank pages,
she reads

From a manuscript of dots. First
a lyric
she has just written

And hastily transcribed—before class—
and another,
"Wishing You Were Here".

Like a passenger waking
aboard a crowded ferryboat
on a frozen lake

My voice
lost in the voices
of the others, I cry out

"Hey, you prodigy
ferryboat Captain,
inventor in the night,

"Who's writing this anyway?"

MR. AMNESIA

Even an amnesiac remembers some things
       better than others.
In one past life I was a subway conductor
for the Chicago subway system.

In another I was—Gosh, I forgot!
Anyway, some years ago, I was run over
by a sports car. Ever since that time

I find I cannot go more than a few days
without leaving my body at least briefly
and then coming back to it. Again and again.

I can't seem to stay in Chicago or in any city,
for that matter, and in one body,
for very long.

I once wrote a forty-nine line poem
made up entirely of first lines, forty-nine beginnings.
"Forty-nine Beginnings" it was called.

I once met a young mother who had gone fishing
with her two children. Coming up from the bottom
of Lake Michigan, I got tangled up in their lines

And they pulled me out and saved my life.
The woman was my wife and the children were
       my children.
"Making love, it's always as if it were happening

"for the first time," I said after ten years of marriage.
"When a woman chooses an amnesiac as her husband,
she has to expect things like that," she laughed.

"Still, there's a lot to be said
for ten years of foreplay."
An Instructor in Modern Poetry, I once lectured

For four weeks as if each class was the first class
of a new year. When the genial Chairman,
manifesting polite alarm,

Visited my classes, the occasion of his being there
gave me the opportunity to teach
as if those classes, too, were new classes.

Promoted, given a raise, a bonus and a new two-year
                    contract,
even I was confused. Each class I taught became one
in an infinite series of semesters, each semester

Lasting no more than fifty minutes.
I don't know about you, but I hardly unpack
and get ready for this lifetime and it's time

To move on to the next. I've been reincarnated
                    three times,
and am forty-nine years old and I don't even know
                    my own name.
History is just one of those things

You learn to live without. I live in a city
the entire population of which is made up of amnesiacs
so for the first time in three lifetimes I feel at home.

YADDO

I'm at Yaddo sheltering myself from the drizzle
          standing under a tree
reading Philip Roth's *The Great American Novel*
waiting for my friends Joe and Carol Bruchac

to arrive
with four friends from Canada
who are in Saratoga Springs, New York,
to give a poetry reading,
Bruce Meyer, Richard Harrison, Robert Lawrence
        and Ross Leckie,
when up pulls this big shiny car
which I approach smiling
thinking it's Joe and Carol,
but it's Burns International
        Security Services, Inc.
and the man wants to know if Yaddo
has anything more than "internal security."
        "I'm John Weidman," he says.
"You must be a writer."
"Yep."
"What's your name?"
"Sward, my name is Robert Sward, like greensward."
"Oh," he says, disappointed he doesn't
know any of my books but
still impressed to be meeting
a Yaddo author.
I should have said, "My name is
Philip Roth, John, and this is my new book,
        The Great American Novel,
but as usual I think of things like that
        too late.
"Look," he says, handing me his business card,
        J.W. Weidman
        Security Sales Consultant,
"Mention my name in your next book, okay?"

PERSONAL STRESS ASSESSMENT

(Found Poem)

Make a list of all the life events that
apply to you ...then add them up with
the points assigned.

To be married and moderately unhappy
is less stressful than to be unmarried
and male and over 30.

To be happily married counts for 0 points.
If your spouse dies that counts for 100 points.
63 for going to jail. 73 for divorce.
Divorce is more stressful than imprisonment.
Getting married is 3 points more stressful
than being fired. Marital reconciliation (45 points)
and retirement (also 45 points)
are only half as stressful as
the death of your spouse.
Minor violations of the law: 11 points.
Trouble with the boss: 23. Christmas: 12. But
sexual difficulties are less stressful
than pregnancy (40 points versus 39).
A mortgage over $10,000 is worse
than a son (or daughter) leaving home.
Trouble with your in-laws is as stressful
as "outstanding personal achievement"
which is only slightly more stressful
than if "wife begins or stops work."

Are you very happy and well-adjusted? 0 points.
Very angry, depressed or frustrated? 20 points.

Conclusion: With 25 points or more, "you probably
will feel better if you reduce your stress."

Half A Life's History, 1983

HALF A LIFE'S HISTORY
(Excerpted from *The Jurassic Shales*)

> Scenario: *An amnesiac wakes one morning*
> *in London, England, in bed with two women. In the*
> *process of recovering his memory, he goes back in*
> *time 160 million years to the Jurassic geological*
> *period to find his true original parents, the first*
> *of the flying dinosaurs. The narrator is himself*
> *a flying dinosaur, and* **The Jurassic Shales** *ends*
> *with his being united with his father and mother.*

Here I am writing to you
half a life's history
"A horse which throws the dreamer to the ground."
I am homesick and America has had a nervous breakdown.
I am taking shaman lessons and studying Karate.
My greatest complaint (you've offered to help) is amnesia.
Do you believe in transmigration of the soul? Yes, I do too.
But what if it can happen not only when one dies, but
        several times in an afternoon?
And I'm sure it's not properly amnesia I am speaking of.
I go out of my body, I come back in.
I say amnesia because sometimes when this happens
        I forget just who I am.
I've been doing this, I believe, with some regularity
        for a quarter of a million years. I'm doing it more
        and more frequently now because I'm unhappy.
        Even the light depresses me. That is, the light
        on Oxford Street, 6 PM on a Sunday. The light
        in Bloom's. The light in Wimpy's. I haven't seen
        light like this since the Middle Ages of the Animals.

We drink, we smoke, we go to parties. Friday night
        we went to the dullest party in 3,000 years
        in Bayswater off the Moscow Road.
I thought the whole time of algae, worms,
        primitive brachiopods, mollusks, crustaceans,
I thought of my mother and those birds with the hollow
        bones.
I am in the library at Swiss Cottage
        eating chocolates in the children's room

What am I reading? Probably I have gone mad.
I am reading up on the eohippus, the first true
    archaic horse.
I identify. Those horses were no larger than dogs.
    I'm a dog and interested in horses
that were once my own size.
Why? I don't know why. Yes, I do. It's because
    I feel I was once (also) a wooly rhinoceros.
That I am at this moment a wooly rhinoceros.
Anyway, I am no longer incapacitated by my erotic
    fantasies.
I am devoting my whole attention to insects, geology, etc.
Each morning I have friends come in to read me my
    biography and my passport.
Then I know who I am. Then I can pay attention
    to what needs to be done.

Who are these people anyway? They think they speak English,
    but I don't understand a word they say.
My only reason for coming was to learn Karate with Kanazawa,
    who has left for Germany.
Oh, I've just gone out of my body and now I'm back.
What is happening in America where, I am convinced,
    in my previous existence, I was a Confederate
    soldier killed in action, 186-?
Well, it doesn't matter. I'll find out soon enough and probably
    know anyway if I'd only think about it.

RETURNING TO LIVE IN 1860

Good morning, 1860.
Good morning.
Good morning, Dr. Whimsy.
Good morning.
Good morning, Beauty.
Truth.
Queen.
Helicopter karma machine.
Industry.
Business machines. Computers.
Simplicity.

Can I have just an hour with the milkmaid?
I want to get back right away then to waging
        the Civil War.
What instructions are there?
Has the Queen left a note? Can I play Lord Shepperton's
        harmonica?
Women being mediums for all I know and for all
        I will ever know (How can I know that, how
        can I assign myself—?)
I want another hour with the milkmaid
and the Queen to read me her diaries and to instruct me
        in every extreme action of which she knows anything.
I want to know the bounds of things and sense,
        and how to cleanse myself.

Is there any peanut butter?
What incredible sticky things are there to eat
        this century?
When did they invent ice-cream?
Anyone carrying on like this is carrying on
        for a reason.
What is the reason?
Where is the child?

But perhaps being forty years before them, I can
        become both my parents' parents.
Has that been done before?
And what if they've gone back forty or even
        sixty years.
What if they're at this moment in the process
        of becoming their own parents?
When will they get to me? When will it be my turn?
I'd like to be present and film my own birth,
to come out with a camera and to be obstetrician,
        my waiting father and Director
        at the same time.
I'd like in fact to be my mother, giving birth
        to an obstetrician-Director-my-waiting
        father and a movie camera.
And to come out with on my wrist
a wrist-sized washing machine, etc., so I could be

immediately fully independent. A stove. Hi-fi.
A library. A hospital with my own
doctors. And a complete set of in-laws.
The question most on my mind:
Where do women come from?
Women come right out of the head of the male god.
Either that or out of the earth—or things about
the earth. People here, there, everywhere, both
ears against it. Listen. Everybody. Alright,
we're listening.

Who are these women with?
Where do they come from?
How do they get that way?

The Bride is with—
the Queen is with—
What about Cassandra? What about Hera?
Are things complementary in more ways even
        than one suspected?
When what happens and what you do
        are the same thing
how is it possible to speak of loving someone or
        wasting time?

I want a banana. I want a tangerine.
I want to rim the most beautiful woman in Manhattan,
        Kansas.
What about Jesus Christ? Where is there a tape
        of him laughing?
In sex, I've found, in loving
the discovery is the cleansing.
I want to swallow it down.
The only sadness is loving
AND NO ILLUMINATION.
Beauty is wallowing.
Loving is practice.
A man having been with a woman, the woman has
        always been there.
Has the man always been there?

SCARF GOBBLE WALLOW INVENTORY

How hungry and for what are the people this season
        predicting the end of the end of the end of
I've only just come home after having been away
The world sends its greetings and the greetings
        send greetings
Hello goodbye, hello goodbye
There are greetings and gifts everywhere
Children screaming and feeling slighted
The next minute we're walking along canals
        on the planet Mars
Twenty minutes later we are earthworms in black
        leather jackets, our pockets filled
        with hamburgers,
Voyage to the moon.
All I am really hungry for is everything
The ability to hibernate and a red suitcase going off
        everywhere
Every cell in your body and every cell in my body is
        hungry and each has its own stomach
Are your cells eating my cells? Whose cell is the
        universe, and what is it sick with, if anything?
Is the universe a womb or a mouth?
And what is hunger, really?
And is the end of the world to be understood in terms of
        hunger or gifts, or the tops of peoples' heads
        coming off?
The most complex dream I've ever dreamed I dreamed
        in London.
It involved in its entirety taking one bite of an orange.

        *   *   *

"What do you want to be when you grow up?" she says.
I'm nearly sixty.
I want to be hungry as I am now and a pediatrician.
The truth is I'm 45 and hungrier than I was when I was
        20 and a sailor.
I'm hungry for ice cream made with ice cream and not
        chemicals or artificial spoons.
I've never been so hungry in my life.

I want one more bacon-lettuce-and-tomato
        sandwich,
to make love and kiss everyone I know goodbye.
Tomorrow at half past four we will all four-and-a-half
        billion of us walk slowly into orbit.
If only one can do this breathing normally, and not trip
        on one's breath or have stomach cramps or clammy
        hands or hysterical needs or a coughing fit or the wish
        to trample or stomp someone, but stepping peacefully
There is ALL the time in the world
There is ALL THE TIME IN THE WORLD
There is all the time in the world.

STATEMENT OF POETICS, or
"GOODBYE TO MYSELF"

I wrote for myself for people.
        I've changed,
I've changed since I began writing
        I write for myself. I believe
more than ever in music, in the sound,
                however gotten, of music
in people's poetry. Rhyme
more than ever. Talk
        people talking, getting that
into one's poetry that
is my poetics. Love
hate lies laughing stealings
self-confession, self-destruction.
No one has to read them. No one
has to publish them.
                I am more
and more for unpublished poetry.
That is why I have a pseudonym, that
is why I now publish poetry.
To hell with the Business
of Anthologies. To hell with Anthologies.

One way and another I have written angry
for twenty years. Now I want music and
the sounds of people.

I want poems that use the word *heart* and
self-confession and incorrect
grammar and the soils and stains of Neruda
and Lorca and Kabir and Williams and
Whitman and Yeats.

Forty-four years old. Stand on my head
ten minutes daily morning
breakfast, supper.
Writing less and less.
Evaporating into the air
feet first. I won't
ever die. I'll simply
stand on my head
and disappear into the
air just like that.

I don't believe in imagination. The prairies
as a landscape are imagination. England is,
as a landscape, a failure of imagination.
Kenya is imagination, India
is reaching even further
than that. And that is why I will
go to India which I will in seven
days time. So this
is a time capsule
in case anyone is
interested and in case
I never come back.

> Goodbye for
> now, goodbye
> goodbye goodbye
> to myself,
> goodbye goodbye
> for now
> goodbye myself,
> goodbye for
> now goodbye.

(1977)

Poet Santa Cruz, 1985

A MONK ON THE SANTA CRUZ MOUNTAINS

—After Ts'en Ts'an

They say there is a monk on the Santa Cruz Mountains,
his white robes floating, three hundred feet beneath
       the sky.
A barefoot, thousand-year-old,
       chocolate-colored genie
who has not spoken in three lifetimes.
His matted, ankle-length hair housed
       a family of scorpions.
Now, small children approach him, dance
and whirl about with his walking stick
which once separated
two demons in a death struggle.

CASTROVILLE, CALIFORNIA—A COFFEE SHOP CUM ART GALLERY

Sonnet

O thistle-like artichoke in the place
of glory. Green peppers: four lushly framed nudes
staring down on us with a kind of greasy grace.
Purple and green eggplants like immodest prudes.

And apples of heroic size, left to right
like paintings of smugly pompous ancestors.
Broccoli plus pale mushrooms in the moonlight,
whitely bulbous omniscient lecturers

On the care and curatorship of fruit
and vegetables which play more a part
in our lives than the sad-eyed, ruling dupes
who clutter up our walls displacing fruits.

I never did before, but now I will:
I sing, dear friends, of brave plain Castroville.

LI PO

(c. 700-760 A.D.)

—after Robert Payne's *The White Pony*

Tall, powerfully built with a loud screeching voice
and bright, hungry tigerish eyes, his black hair
flowing over his shoulders.
The high heavenly priest of the white lake
with murderers and thieves for ancestors.
Musician, swordsman and connoisseur of fine wines,
        a drunk, a murderer—
Mr. Fairyland, Mr. Landscape of an
         impossible flowering.
He was called a god in exile, the great phoenix
whose wings obscure the sun.
"I am strong enough," boasted this poet, "to meet
ten thousand men."

Li Po who, at death, was summoned by angelic hosts,
who rode off on the backs of dolphins
and, led by the two children of immortality,
entered the celestial palace in triumph.

THE EMPEROR

A villanelle

From *The Way And Its Power*

The world as seen in vision has no name;
call it the Sameness or the Mystery
or rather the "Darker than any Mystery."

Fan Li who, offered half a kingdom,
stepped into a light boat and was heard from
no more. The world as seen in vision has no name.

An empty vessel that one draws from
without its ever needing to be filled. The name-
less, the darker than any Mystery.

Can you love people, rule the land,
yet remain unknown? Play always the female part?
The world as seen in vision has no name.

Rear them, feed them, but do not lay claim.
He who in dealing with the empire,
darker than any mystery,

Regards his high rank as though it were
his body, is the best person to be entrusted with rule.
The world as seen in vision has no name;
call it the Darker than any Mystery.

Four Incarnations, 1991

Foreword:

FOUR INCARNATIONS

Born on the Jewish North Side of Chicago, *bar mitzvahed*, sailor, amnesiac, university professor (Cornell, Iowa, Connecticut College), newspaper editor, food reviewer, father of five children, husband to four wives, my writing career has been described by critic Virginia Lee as a "long and winding road."

1. Switchblade Poetry: Chicago Style

I began writing poetry in Chicago at age 15, when I was named corresponding secretary for a gang of young punks and hoodlums called the Semcoes. A Social Athletic Club, we met at various locations two Thursdays a month. My job was to write postcards to inform my brother thugs—who carried switchblade knives and stole cars for fun and profit—as to when, where and why we were meeting.

Rhyming couplets seemed the appropriate form to notify characters like light-fingered Foxman, cross-eyed Harris, and Irving "Koko," of upcoming meetings. My switchblade juvenilia:

> *The Semcoes meet next Thursday night*
> > *at Speedway*
> *Koko's. Five bucks dues, Foxman, or fight.*

Koko, a young boxer. his father owned Chicago's Speedway Wrecking Company, basement filled with punching bags and pinball machines. Koko and the others joked about my affliction—the writing of poetry—but were so astonished that they criticized me mainly for my inability to spell.

2. Sailor Librarian: San Diego

At 17, I graduated from high school, gave up my job as soda jerk and joined the Navy. The Korean War was underway; my mother had died, and Chicago seemed an oppressive place to be.

My thanks to the U.S. Navy. They taught me how to type (60 words a minute), organize an office, and serve as a librarian. In 1952 I served in Korea aboard a 300-foot long, flat-bottomed Landing Ship Tank (LST). A Yeoman 3rd Class, I became overseer of 1200 paperback books, a sturdy upright typewriter, and a couple of filing cabinets.

The best thing about duty on an LST is the ship's speed: 8-10 knots. It takes approximately one month for an LST to sail between San Diego and Pusan, Korea.In that month I read Melville's *Moby Dick*, Whitman's *Leaves of Grass*, Thoreau's *Walden*, Isak Dinesen's *Winter's Tales*, the King James Version of the Bible, Shakespeare's *Hamlet*, *King Lear*, and a biography of Abraham Lincoln.

While at sea, I began writing poetry as if poems, to paraphrase Thoreau, were secret letters from some distant land.

I sent one poem to a girl named Lorelei with whom I was in love. Lorelei had a job at the Dairy Queen. Shortly before enlisting in the Navy, I spent $15 of my soda jerk money taking her up in a single engine, sight-seeing airplane so we could kiss and—at the same time—get a good look at Chicago from the air. Beautiful Loreli never responded to my poem. Years later, at the University of Iowa Writers' Workshop, I learned that much of what I had been writing (love poems inspired by a combination of lust and loneliness) belonged, loosely speaking, to a tradition—the venerable tradition of unrequited love.

3. Mr. Amnesia: Cambridge

In 1962, after ten years of writing poetry, my book, *Uncle Dog & Other Poems,* was published by Putnam in England. That was followed by two books from Cornell University Press, *Kissing the Dancer* and *Thousand-Year-Old Fiancée*. Then in 1966, I was invited to do 14 poetry readings in a two-week stretch at places like Dartmouth, Amherst, and the University of Connecticut.

The day before I was scheduled to embark on the reading series, I was hit by a speeding MG in Cambridge, Massachusetts.

I lost my memory for a period of about 24 hours. Just as I saw the world fresh while cruising to a war zone, so I now caught a glimpse of what a city like Cambridge can look like when one's inner slate, so to speak, is wiped clean.

4. Santa Claus: Santa Cruz

In December, 1985, recently returned to the U.S. after some years in Canada, a free lance writer in search of a story, I sought and found employment as a Rent-a-Santa Claus. Imagine walking into the local Community Center and suddenly, at the sight of 400 children, feeling transformed from one's skinny, sad-eyed self, into an elf—having to chant the prescribed syllables, "Ho, Ho, Ho."

What is poetry? For me, it's the restrained music of a switchblade knife. It's an amphibious warship magically transformed into a basketball court, and then transformed again into a movie theater showing a film about the life of Joan of Arc. It is the vision of an amnesiac, bleeding from a head injury, witnessing the play of sunlight on a redbrick wall.

Poetry comes to a bearded Jewish wanderer, pulling on a pair of high rubber boots with white fur, and a set of musical sleigh bells, over blue, fleece-lined sweat pants. It comes to the father of five children bearing gifts for 400 and, choked up, unable to speak, alternately laughing and sobbing the three traditional syllables—Ho, Ho, Ho—hearing at the same time, in his heart, the more plaintive, tragic—*Oi vay, Oi vay, Oi vay.*

CLANCY THE DOG

—For Claire

He is so ugly he is a psalm to ugliness,
this extra-terrestrial, short-haired
midget sea-lion,
snorts, farts, grunts, turns somersaults
on his mistress' bed.

She calls him an imperfect Boston terrier,
part gnome, part elf,
half something and half something else,
180,000,000-year-old Clancy
with his yellowy-white, pin-pointy teeth
and red, misshapen pre-historic gums.

Clancy has no tail at all and doesn't bark.
He squeaks like a monkey,
flies through the air,
lands at six every morning
on his mistress' head,
begging to be fed and wrapped not in a robe
but a spread.

Tree frog, wart hog, ground hog,
"Clancy, Clancy," she calls for him
in the early morning fog,
and he appears, anything, anything,
part anything, but a dog.

SCARLET THE PARROT

Scarlet perches on the office windowsill
shrieking, hollering, barking

Like a dog. She knocks her mottled beak
against the warehouse window

And tries to open
the metal hook and eye latch.

There are parrot droppings
on the telephone and Scarlet has eaten

Part of the plastic receiver.
The parrot slides like a red fireman

With yellow and blue feathers
up and down the cord,
        holding on

With her beak, maneuvering gracefully
        with her claws.
When I approach she calls, "Hello, hello…"

Walks up my trouser leg holding on
with her macaw's beak. I feed the bird

Oranges and pears, almonds
and sunflower seeds.

I swivel my head round and round
in imitation of her neck movements.

"What's happening?" she asks,
and again, "What's happening?"

"Hello, cookie. Yoo-hoo…
Can you talk, can you talk?" she asks

Chewing for several minutes,
finally swallowing
            a leather button

Off my green corduroy jacket, threatening,
ready to tear my ear off,

Biting if I place my finger
in her mouth. Her tongue is black

And her beady eyes piercing like an eagle's.
She wants a response, tests my reactions.

Tenderly the parrot walks up my corduroy jacket,
sensually restraining her claws. I'm aroused.

When a dog barks, she barks too: *Rrf, rrf.*
Casually, a relaxed but authentic

Imitation. "Hello, darling," she breathes,
looking me in the eye knowing I know

If it pleases her she might bite my ear off.
"Yoo-hoo, yoo-hoo, now you say something," she says.

THE APTERYX (1/35) OF WEBSTER'S DICTIONARY—
AND NEW ZEALAND

The inflected apteryx (or kiwi) would appear
to be a rudimentary, an essentially
Webster-bird. The apteryx (from the Greek a +
Pteryx) does not fly, and, in fact
lacks all regard (and need) for flight.

Flat-breastboned, hen-sized and scratchy,
the apteryx stands on two, declining
and unlikely chicken legs. It *ooou's* for food
through a long, thin reed-like beak:
insects, snails, crippled fleas and berries.

Its nostrils are at the last half-inch of its beak.
And the bird—not quite extinct—survives
under government protection. It reproduces
slowly, and in public, burrow-hiding.

If its hairs were feathers, ocellated
aphrodisiacal, the sleepy—marginal—asterisk-eyed
apteryx... could (conceivably) strut, cock
and play the peacock; however, with its one hint
of a tail, and grayish, short shag-brown hair

The apteryx would seem content to *ooou*. And,
its beak alone, apt & straight, endears it
to one; —but when it curls itself, extinct
within its sleeping back (by day)
enwhiskering its *ooou*, the apteryx returns
upon the government and Webster of it all.

ALFA THE DOG

It isn't enough that when I go off for three weeks to an
artists' colony and phone home, the first thing my wife
tells me is there's a new addition to the family, a seven-
month-old poodle named Alfa and that Alfa has papers,
an honest-to-God pedigree that includes not only aristo-
cratic ancestors, but recent appearances in "The New York
Review of Books" and a novel published by Houghton-
Mifflin. And when I am somewhat less than ecstatic,
my wife asks me to at least say a few words to the new
addition, and puts on Alfa the dog. "Speak, Alfa, speak,"
I hear her say. And Alfa who is, by all accounts, loyal
and obedient, a noted storyteller, intelligent and amusing
as Oscar Wilde, refuses to speak, to bark, or make some
witty remark like, "What's the weather like in Saratoga?"
All I hear is Alfa's low doggy breathing and the tinkle
of the elegant silver bell on her collar.

My wife comes back on and says, "I have an idea. You
bark into the phone. Alfa will answer back."

Well, it's only costing a dollar ninety-five a minute and
good-natured soul that I am, devoted to my wife, guilty
at running off for three weeks, I put myself into it, throw
back my head and howl, barking, yowling, yipping like a
real dog—a dog without papers, a dog with fleas, a dog
like one of those mutts I knew growing up in Chicago,
and this happening, of course, on the public pay phone
at Yaddo, the "artists' heaven," what the New York *Times*
calls the Harvard of Artists' Colonies.

Looking up, sure enough, I see one of America's more
distinguished composers with his mouth open, his pipe
falling to the floor, waiting in line, no doubt, to speak
to his wife and children and his cats and dogs.

"Well, darling," I say, "we've been talking for twenty-
five minutes. This is going to cost a fortune."

At that moment, Alfa decides she wants to make her
presence known to all concerned, and she begins barking
into the phone, answering me in kind, responding yip
for yip, and yap for yap, lest there be any doubt in
anyone's mind as to who it is I have been speaking—
me to Alfa the dog, Alfa the dog to me.

THREE ROBERTS

From heart to heart
from brain to brain
from Robert to Robert

Robert Zend phones Robert
Sward. *Ring, ring.*
"Robert, this is Robert."

"Is this Robert?" "This
is Robert, Robert." "Yes,
Robert?" I say, "This

"Is Robert, too." "Ah,
excuse me, I need
to find a match,"

Says Robert Zend putting
down the telephone
and rummaging for matches,

Granting me, a non-smoker,
the status of accessory
to his addiction.

All this occurring a few
seconds into an otherwise
scintillating conversation.

"I had a very pleasant afternoon
while reading your poems,"
Margaret Trudeau once remarked

About Zend's book, *From Zero To One,*
and I can fully understand
her saying that.

Zend translates serious things
into funny things
and funny things

Into serious things.
He also translates himself
into other people, and

Other people into himself—
and where does one of us end
and the other begin?

And where does Zend begin
and where do I zend?
I mean, end?

And what about Robert Priest?
Is he a visible man,
an invisible man?

Or the man who broke out of the Letter X?
Is he a spaceman in disguise?
A blue pyramid? A golden trumpet?

A chocolate lawnmower?
An inexhaustible flower?
Or a reader who escaped

From some interstellar library?
Rock Musician in residence
at the University of the Moon?

And meanwhile Robert Zend
looks into his mirror
and sees not Zend

But Chicago-born Uncle Dog;
Half a Life's History;
Mr. Amnesia; Mr. Movies: Left To Right;

Mr. Transmigration of the Soul;
the poet as wanderer;
a forty-nine-year-old human violin...

Robert Zend the Nomad
gazing in like an acrobat
at the window in the sky.

Ring, ring. "Robert, this
is Robert." "Is this Robert?"
"This is Robert, Robert."

"Yes, Robert," I say speaking
to my friend Robert One,
"This is Robert Two."

Roberts...
Robertness...
Three Knights of a Roberthood.

BASKETBALL'S THE AMERICAN GAME BECAUSE IT'S HYSTERICAL

"Basketball's the American game because it's hysterical,"
says Lorrie Goldensohn as the players and coaches come
off the bench and the crowd is on its feet yelling and
the Knicks are ahead 97-95 with just over three minutes
to go in the fourth quarter and Perry hits from the side
and Lorrie's husband, Barry, comes downstairs with a
bottle of scotch and a guide to English verse.

"Unless there is
a new mind, there cannot be a new line," he reads
refilling our glasses.
"Without invention the line
will never again take on its ancient
divisions…"

All evening we have been watching the New York Knicks
battling the Boston Celtics and having a running
argument about free verse, traditional rhyming poetry,
syllabic verse ("what's the point in counting for
counting's sake?"), the critic Hugh Kenner, John
Hollander's *Rhyme's Reason,* the variable foot and
the American idiom.

"In and out by Williams," says the announcer, "he's got
a nose for the basket." The crowd is on its feet
again, roaring.

"We know nothing and can know nothing
but the dance, to dance to a measure
contrapuntally,
Satyrically, the tragic foot," Barry continues.

The Celtics race down the court. "Talk about the
green wave coming at you." Bird hits and the Celtics
even the score.

"Basketball's the American game because it's like the
variable foot," says Lorrie, "it's up in the air
all the time. It's quick and the floor is continually
moving and there's this short back and forth factor."

"What I like best about the game," I say, "is shutting
my eyes and tuning out the announcer and hearing
Barry read and arguing about poetry and drinking
and listening all the while to the music of
seven-foot black herons in gym shoes, ten giant
gazelles, the stirring squeak of twenty over-size
sneakers on the varnished floor, a floor which
has been carefully and ingeniously miked in advance
for sound."

ON MY WAY TO THE KOREAN WAR...

—For President Dwight Eisenhower

On my way to the Korean war,
I never got there.
One summer afternoon in 1952,
I stood instead in the bow
of the Attack Transport *Menard,*
with an invading force
of 2,000 battle-ready Marines,
watching the sun go down.
Whales and porpoises,
flying fish and things jumping
out of the water.
Phosphoresence—
Honolulu behind us,
Inchon, Korea, and the war ahead.

Crewcut, 18-year-old librarian,
Yeoman 3rd Class, editor
of the ship's newspaper,
I wrote critically if unoriginally
of our Commander-in-Chief,
Mr. President,
and how perplexing it was that he
would launch a nuclear-powered submarine
while invoking the Lord,
Crocodile Earthshaker,
Shiva J. Thunderclap,
choosing the occasion to sing
the now famous *Song of the Armaments,*
the one with the line "weapons for peace":

> O weapons for peace,
> O weapons for peace,
> awh want, awh want
> more weapons for peace!

At sundown, a half dozen sailors
converged on the bow of the ship
where, composed and silent,

we'd maintain our vigil
until the sun had set.

Careful to avoid being conspicuous,
no flapping or flailing of the arms,
no running, horizontal take-offs,
one man, then another, stepped out into space,
headed across the water,
moving along as if on threads.
After a while, I did the same:
left my body just as they left theirs.

In-breathe, out-breathe, and leave,
in-breathe, out-breathe, and leave.
Leave your body, leave your body,
leave your body, leave your body,

we sang as we went out
to where the light went,
and whatever held us to that ship
and its 2,000 battle-ready troops, let go.
So it was, dear friends, I learned to fly.
And so in time must you
and so will the warships,
and the earth itself,
and the sky,
for as the prophet says, the day cometh
when there will be no earth left to leave.

O me, O my,
O me, O my,
goodbye earth, goodbye sky.
Goodbye, goodbye.

1950s / 1960s

Pre-med
        thinking he's
got to learn about the world
all over again from
        square one

Doesn't think he knows anything for sure
only the hula hoops and Twinkies,
the blues and violets of his mind
        very late at night

        red and pink lipstick case
with a little mirror on one side,
hat, stockings, garter belt
        and gloves

He bought a shirt in 1950 the most remarkable
        feature of which is
that a snag or tear will reduce it
        to nothing.

It's a shirt made of a single cell
that, when it's reduced to nothing,
a single cell remains.
        The original cell of that fabric.

What he is seeking is a quilt
made up of the original cells of all the fabrics.

What the 1950s does
like a blow to the back or side of one's head
it relocates your mind

                *   *   *

'Delicious' apples and the popularity of DDT

James Dean
Peter Lawford,
Elizabeth Taylor,
        the Mickey Mouse Club
                taken seriously

The time many people who came into their own
        in the 1960s
first got laid

The Rosenberg's frying in the electric chair
      McCarthy and his crony Roy Cohn
the atomic bomb already five years old

Nixon: "California politics is a can of worms"
Captain Kangaroo, Howdy Doody

          *   *   *

Inhaling
The jazz was good
Death was softened, advancements made
in the salesmanship of everything

His own deepest impulses
      were not to nurse or nurture
      but to hang out again
at Sonny Berkowitz' Pool Hall,
wearing blue suede shoes,
Levis and navy blue shirt.
He bought a zip gun,
joined a street gang

Once, joint in hand,
exploring the intricacies
of the Chicago Drainage Canal,
he entered a sewer
and ambled deeply as he could
reflecting all the while
on his chances of surviving
the synchronized flushing
of three-and-a-half million toilets.

For the first time in 2,000 years
one went four years to a University
without hearing one true word;
going to work for Hallmark Greeting cards
or the phone company
one knew something was at hand because things
became easy.

Tin-Pan alley
people in college dormitories subscribing
        to *Photoplay*
and *The Nail Polish Review*.

>   Five foot two, eyes of blue,
>   cotton candy hair
>   fluffy lavender
>   angora sweater
>   short white socks
>   with fat cuffs
>   one of a hundred couples
>   in a Champaign, Illinois
>   dormitory lounge.

>   *Rock Hudson singing to Doris Day,*
>   *...beautiful girl,*
>   *your eyes, your hair*
>   *is beyond compare...*
>   *(Pillow Talk)*

>   "Touch me, touch me,"
>   guiding his hand
>   into her pleated wool skirt,
>   'petting' it was called,
>   one foot touching the floor at all times
>   ejaculating
>   somewhere or other
>   somehow or other
>   discreetly as possible
love in the 1950s.

He sees giant mushroom cloud
father of the H-Bomb Edward Teller

>   *an entire island,*
>   *Eniwetok,*
>   *radioactive coral dust*
>   *a gigantic cauliflower, blue and gray*
>   *and mauve...*
>   *five million tons of TNT*

Police Action Korea Harry Truman
and Dwight David Eisenhower,
each with six legs and arms
dancing to the music
of Lord Shiva and Judy Garland
doing it
on a pink velvet loveseat

some twenty-five miles into the stratosphere,
and spread a hundred miles across the sky.

ODE TO TORPOR

Glory be to God for the tiresome and tedious,
Glory be to God for tedium,
for no news about anything,

for newspaper strikes and power outages,
lethargy and downtime.

Postpone and delay. And again,
postpone and delay.
No place to go. No way to get there.
No reason not to stay.

Glory be to God for inaction,
for not getting things done,
for not getting anything done,

No huffin', no puffin',
just some of that slow and easy,
the woman lackadaisically on top,
the man lackadaisically on top.
Yummy, yummy, take your time,
yummy, yummy, I'll take mine.

Slow and easy,
slow and easy.
Glory be to God, O glory.

O glory be to God.

CONTINUOUS TOPLESS STRIPPERS

An eight-speaker sound system,
two continuous topless strippers,
Elvis Presley singing *Early Morning Rain*.

Everyone loves television.
And because the management doesn't want
to offend anyone's tastes by omitting

So important an element
in the desired sensory mix—
"The lowest common denominator

"Creates an art form," my friend
mutters into his beer—
the five foot by seven foot color TV

Is seen on stage backing up the strippers,
the TV little more than a concentration
of bright flashing lights which,

On closer examination, turn out
to be the Six o'clock Evening News.
"Some damn half-deranged diplomat,

"Portfolio this, portfolio that,
is dithering about something or other somewhere
or other for no reason that neither you nor I

"Nor anyone else has any idea." My friend
orders another, and I order another.
The announcer, meanwhile, is selling hangover

Or headache pills and the difficulty we all have
on occasion of falling asleep or eliminating
properly or what happens when we drink too much
     coffee

And that and everything else at last dissolves
the dancers achieving what appears, in fact, to be
a new breakthrough

In negotiations, winning
in the ovation that follows
their performance

Not only our freedom
but the release and freedom
of all hostages.

SAUSALITO FERRY POEM

"Okay, we're here! Stop scribbling,"
she shouts back at me
climbing down the iron ladder
expecting me to follow.

The boat goes sailing off
to Tiburon,
me with one-half a new poem standing
waving at her from the railing.

"Pink light round your white body,
your blue eyes flashing," I sing
into the wind.
"What's that you're saying? I forgot
to get off?
It's all over now between us?

"All I care about is poetry?
O listen, my love, just listen.
You know that's not true.
I know you'll like this one,
these lines
written exclusively for you."

108,000 WAYS OF MAKING LOVE

Her lips are full, magenta-red
      in color—

Bare-chested, she wears a yellow silk
      loin cloth.
I cup my right hand
      under her blue chin
and bend to kiss her,
encircling her waist with my left arm.

Her back to me, she turns

Strings of pearls,
lion-claw necklaces and
rubies and gold round her neck.

Her skin is dark,
      dark as the skin of the blue god.
She has thick, reddish-brown hair
      and brown eyes.

She's wearing garlands
      of fresh wild flowers,
gold rings on every finger,
      red and golden bangles
carved like serpents round
      both ankles.

I stroke her pearly, iridescent thighs,
tenderly smacking
      as she tenderly slaps and smacks me back,

Our bodies etched with scratches
      of our sharp nails

...hooting and chirruping
with the brazen night birds
gazing in at us
from half-open windows
and doorways

Framed by purple, green,
red-pink twilit bougainvillea.

She presses her big toe
and also her next
to biggest toe, and the toe
next to that, and all her other toes,
high up into my crotch
as I gently guide her with my hand.

I enter her with my mouth
and she with her mouth
does the same
as I enter her from the front
and behind,
even as she lowers herself onto my body,
even as I rise to pull her
to me.
Mirrors installed in the ceilings and walls
illustrate what we dedicate ourselves to:

Making love in 108,000 ways
all at the same time.

KISS BITE AND MOO SOFTLY

—*Muse voice is loved woman mumbling.*

Going shopping with the muse
you come away buying the right things:
rare books and cashmere pullovers for him,
silk dresses, a gold and amethyst necklace for her.
Her skin
fair and fine as the yellow
lotus, eyes bright as orbs
of a fawn, well-cut with reddish
corners. Bosom hard,
full and high, neck
goodly shaped as the conch
shell. Love seed. Kama
salila, the water of life.
Swan-like gait. Note

of the Kokila-bird. Kisses
don't interrupt sentences.
 Sleeping
her arms fall into the same
position
 as the Statue of Liberty.

JEALOUSY

She buys a green corduroy jacket
with a velvet collar
and a label that reads
 Crazy Horse

But tries it on first in the fitting room
where I pull her to me,
reaching up
 under her blouse,
nuzzling her breasts,
stroking her back,
my hands jealous of my lips,
my lips jealous of my hands

I tell her of my jealousy, and she confesses
to an urge to call me on the phone
at that time of the afternoon
when I'm likely to be at home.

She becomes annoyed
 at my unfaithfulness,
that instead of being there to answer the phone
I lie beside her,
 stroking
 exploring
our lips joined,
until at last
rolling together on the fitting room floor—

"I want to speak with you," she breathes,
"and have you all to myself,
I want to hear you call for me and moan.
Lover, oh lover," she sighs at last
"I want to call now and tell my lover,
 oh, my lover, oh, my lover."

48 POETS NAMED ROBERT

1.

Yes, I met Robert Frost and Robert Lowell and Robert Creeley,
Robert Duncan, Robert Mezey, Robert Bly, Robert Peterson,
appeared in *A Controversy of Poets, An Anthology of
Contemporary American Poetry* edited by Robert Kelly,
but not in *New Poets of England and America* edited by Robert
Pack, admire the work of Robert Bridges, Robert Browning, Robert
Burns, Bobbie Creeley, Robert Dana, Robert Finch, Roberto Galvan,
Robert Graves, Robert Hass, Robert Herrick, Robert Hogg, Yo!
Bob Holman, Robert Huff, Robert Kroetsch, Robert Lax, Robbie
McCauley, Robert McGovern, Roberta Mandel, Robert Peters,
Robert Pinsky, Robert Southey, Robert Louis Stevenson and
Roberto Vargas, and even performed in taverns and coffee
houses in London, Ontario, and in Toronto at Major Robert's
Restaurant—near the intersection of Major and Robert Street—
with Canadian poets Robert Priest and Robert Zend, the three of us,
billed as the Three Roberts, dedicating our readings to CBC Radio's
Robert Weaver and Robert Prowse, to the critic Robert Fulford,
with half a dedication to our friend John Robert Colombo, and to Robert
Service.

2.

But as each of my four wives explained, patiently or otherwise,
over a period of four decades, "Robert, it doesn't pay. Robert,
there's no future in it. I'm not going to go on like this..." and
"Robert, doesn't it depress you to go into libraries and see all
those books by all those other writers named Robert, even
the ones not named Robert, that practically no one on earth
is going to read?" Well, yes, it's true it doesn't pay. And it's true
there's no future in it. And it does depress me that practically
no one in America reads poetry, and that is why I took a job
writing software user manuals after teaching for fourteen years.
But then, unable to let go of what I'd done, resigned in order
to go back and write more poetry. And today I think
of you all as I re-read mail from 1984, the year I left Canada.

Three letters. One from Robert Priest, the Canadian poet.
He writes of the death by drowning of Robert B.,

and the deaths also of poets not named Robert.
And Earle 'Robert' Birney, he says, who, at 75 was seen
by the editor of *New: American & Canadian Poetry*
in a Toronto rainstorm in the throes of love running up
Yonge Street bearing flowers for his 35-year-old sweetheart;
Birney who, at 79 fell out of a tree from which
he'd been trying to dislodge a kite, and who, not long after,
recovering from an injured hip, resumed cycling
on a regular basis at breakneck speed through a North
Toronto cemetery; Birney, he says, alive and in his 80s,
had visitors who read him his poems, poems that,
when Birney heard them, with impaired memory,
he enjoyed, though he was unable to understand
he was the author of those poems.

Letter #2: Nicky 'Bob' Drumbolis, proprietor
of a Toronto bookstore, writes that his rent has gone up
$700 a month, that he must give up the store, and
that he is 'earnestly clearing stock for the big move.'

And Roberto 'Robbie' Roberts, a publisher, writes
that he has become part owner of Omega Apparel,
a business to which he now devotes all his time. He's not
doing any more poetry these days, only neckties.

3.

I drift off at my computer and dream of Robert Zend,
whose heart gave out that same year and of Robert Priest
and Robert Graves, and in the dream I see myself reading
my favorite Graves poems to Graves, and he is lucid as
my father before his heart stopped at 82, and just before I wake,
Graves tells me I am a cross between Halley's comet and Rip
Van Winkle the way I go off to England, France, Mexico,
Canada, and then, years later, return, meeting the
sons and daughters of the people, of the Roberts I once knew,
and that that is what poems are supposed to do,
and that I have been living more like a poem than a man
with his feet on the ground, and that in the time that remains
I should be living more like a man with his feet on the ground
and less like a poem.

FOR GLORIA ON HER 60TH BIRTHDAY, OR LOOKING FOR LOVE IN MERRIAM-WEBSTER

"Beautiful, splendid, magnificent,
delightful, charming, appealing,"
       says the dictionary.
And that's how I start... But I hear her say,
"Make it less glorious and more Gloria."

Imperious, composed, skeptical, serene,
lustrous, irreverent,
she's marked by glory, she attracts glory
"Glory," I say, "Glory, Glory."

"Is there a hallelujah in there?"
she asks, when I read her lines one and two.
"Not yet," I say, looking up from my books.
She protests, "Writing a poem isn't the same

"As really attending to me." "But it's for
your birthday," I say. Pouting,
playfully cross, "That's the price you pay
when your love's a poet."

She has chestnut-colored hair,
old fashioned Clara Bow lips,
moist brown eyes...
          arms outstretched, head thrown back
she glides toward me and into her seventh decade.

Her name means "to adore,"
"to rejoice, to be jubilant,
to magnify and honor as in worship, to give or ascribe glory—"
      my love, O Gloria, I do, I do.

Rosicrucian in the Basement, 2001

*To a foot in a shoe, the whole world seems paved with
leather.*

—The Hitopadesa, c. 500 A.D.

1. ROSICRUCIAN IN THE BASEMENT

i.
"What's to explain?" he asks.
He's a closet meditator. Rosicrucian in the basement.
In my father's eyes: dream.
"There are two worlds," he says,
  liquid-filled crystal flask
              and yellow glass egg
on the altar.
He's the "professional man" —
        so she calls him, my stepmother.
That, and "the Doctor":
"The Doctor will see you now," she says,
        working as his receptionist.
He's podiatrist—foot surgery a specialty—
        on Chicago's North Side.
Russian-born Orthodox Jew
        with *zaftig* Polish wife, posh silvery white starlet
        Hilton Hotel hostess.

ii.
This is his secret.
This is where he goes when he's not making money.
The way to the other world is into the basement
and he can't live without this other world.
"If he has to, he has to," my stepmother shrugs.
Keeps door locked when he's not down there.
Keeps the door locked when he is.
"Two nuts in the mini-bar," she mutters, banging pots
        in the kitchen upstairs.
Anyway, she needs to protect the family.
"Jew overboard," she yells, banging dishes.
"Peasant!" he yells back.

iii.
"There are two worlds," he says lighting incense, "the seen
and the unseen, and she doesn't understand.
This is my treasure," he says,
        lead cooking in an iron pan,
liquid darkness and some gold.

"Son, there are three souls: one, the Supernal;
        two, the concealed
                female soul, soul like glue…
holds it all together…"
"And the third?" I ask.
We stand there: "I can't recall."
He begins to chant and wave incense.
No *tallis,* no *yarmulke,*
just knotty pine walls and mini-bar
        size of a ouija board,
a little schnapps and shot glasses
on the lower shelf,
and I'm no help.
Just back from seven thousand dollar trip,
four weeks with Swami Muktananda,
                thinking
Now there's someone who knew how to convert
the soul's longing into gold.
Father, my father: he has this emerald tablet
        with a single word written on it
and an arrow pointing.

2. JESUS

"What is it with the cross? You believe in Jesus, dad?"
"What?"
"Are you still a Jew?"
He turns away.
"Dammit, it's not a religion, *verstehst?*"
        Brings fist down on the altar.
"We seek the perfection of metals," he says,
        re-lighting stove,
                "salvation by smelting."

"But what's the point?" I ask.

"The point? Internal alchemy, *shmegegge. Rosa mystica,*" he shouts.
Meat into spirit, darkness into light."

Seated now, seated on bar stools.
Flickering candle in a windowless room.
Visible and invisible. Face of my father

in the other world.
I see him, see him in me
my rosy cross
                podiatrist father.
"I'm making no secret of this secret," he says,
turning to the altar.
"Tell me, tell me how to pray."
"Burst," he says, "burst like a star."

3. ROSY CROSS FATHER

Mother:
  "Yes, he still believes. Imagine—
        American Jews,
                when they die,
roll underground for three days
to reach the Holy Land.
He believes that."

We're standing at the Rosicrucian mini-bar listening,
                father
        with thick, dark-rimmed glasses
blue-denim shirt,
        bristly white mustache,
        and dome forehead.

"Your stepmother's on the phone with her sister," he says.

"He thinks he can look into the invisible,"
        she says from above.
"He thinks he can peek into the other world,
like God's out there waiting for him...
Meshugge!"

She starts the dishwasher.

"As above, so below," he says.
"I'm not so sure," I say.
"Listen, everyone's got some stink," he says,
        grabbing my arm,
                "you think you're immune?"
I shake my head.

"To look for God is to find Him," he says.
"If God lived on earth," she says, "people would knock out
        all His windows."
"Kibbitzer," he yells back. *"Gottenyu! Shiksa brain!"*

Father turns to his "apparatus,"
"visual scriptures," he calls them,
        tinctures and elixirs,
        the silvery dark and the silvery white.

"We of the here-and-now, pay our respects
to the invisible.
                Your soul is a soul," he says, turning to me,
"but body is a soul, too. As the poet says,
'we are the bees of the golden hive of the invisible.'"
"What poet, Dad?"
"The poet! Goddammit, the poet," he yells.

He's seventy-one, paler these days, showing more forehead,
        thinning down.

"We live in darkness and it looks like light.
Now listen to me: I'm unhooking from the world, understand?
Everything is a covering,
contains its opposite.
The demonic is rooted in the divine.
Son, you're an Outside," he says,
        "waiting for an Inside.
but I want you to know..."
"Know what, Dad?"
"I'm gonna keep a place for you in the other world."

THE PODIATRIST'S SON

When our feet hurt, we hurt all over.
                                    —Socrates

1. The Podiatrist's Son

Mother:
"One day the kid will wake up,
          come down to earth
and enroll
          at the Illinois College of Podiatry."

                    Father:
                    "But look, his feet aren't on the
                    ground."

"They've never been on the ground. He's a dreamer."

                    "Just look at that posture! And he toes
                    in. Poor feet, poor posture. The boy
                    lives in another world."

"Wait, I think he needs a new pair of shoes."

                    "Oxfords, shoes that will support him,
                    shoes with laces,
                    shoes that breathe."

"Listen. Listen to your father," she says.

2. How To Shop For Shoes

                    "No loafers, no sandals, nothing
                    without laces," he says.

                    "There are fifty-two bones in the feet;
                    thirty-three joints; more than one
                    hundred tendons, muscles and
                    ligaments..."

We're on our way to Jackson's Shoes.

"Fit for length, fit for width,
get both feet fitted.

"People are asymmetrical. You'll find
one foot, one testicle, one breast
larger than the other…"

"Listen, listen to your father," she says.

"Feet swell, grow larger
as the day goes on.

"So, nu? shop when they're bigger,
shop for the larger foot.

"Otherwise…
heel pain, heel spurs, bunions and
hammertoes…

"Remember, there's no break in
period, shoes don't break in.
Buy what feels right now."

"Listen, listen to your father."

3. *Getting Through the Night*

"So: the foot is the mirror of health.
What's that smell?
Let me see your feet. *Oi!*

"How many times do I have to say it?
A pair of feet have twenty-five
thousand sweat glands, can produce
eight ounces, a cup of perspiration in a
single day.

"One quarter of all the bones in the
human body are in the feet."

He sits at my bedside carving arch supports.

> "Take a flashlight.
> Never walk around in the dark.
> Most foot fractures occur at night…

> "Now remember your slippers," he says
> as I head for the bathroom.

In my father's house
there are no bedtime stories.

ONE-STOP FOOT SHOP

"We walk with angels
and they are our feet.

"'Vibrating energy packets,'" he calls them. "'Bundles of soul
in a world of meat.' Early warning system—
dry skin and brittle nails;
feelings of numbness and cold;
these are symptoms; they mean something.
I see things physicians miss.

"All you have to do is open your eyes, just open your eyes,
and you'll see: seven-eighths of everything is invisible, a spirit
inside the spirit.
The soul is rooted in the foot.
As your friend Bly says, 'The soul longs to go down';
feet know the way to the other world,
that world where people are awake.
So do me a favor: dream me no dreams.
A dreamer is someone who's asleep.

"You know, the material world is infinite,
but boring infinite," he says, cigarette in hand,
little wings fluttering at his ankles.

"And women," he says, smacking his head,
"four times as many foot problems as men.
High heels are the culprit.

"I may be a podiatrist, but I know what I'm about:
feet. Feet don't lie,

     don't cheat, don't kiss ass. Truth is,
peoples' feet are too good for them."

GOOD NEWS FROM THE OTHER WORLD

Palm Springs, CA

"Dad, you're lookin' good," I say,
"like the fountain of youth."

His hands on my feet, grimacing, weary,
mercurial, wing-footed
eighty-year-old doctor.

Wears a denim shirt, bola tie,
turquoise and silver tip,
tanned, tennis-playing, macho…

"Making more money now,
more than in Skokie.
But you need arch supports," he says,
encasing my feet in plaster.

Damaged feet. Feet out of alignment.
Four-times married, forty-year-old feet.

"Well, good news from the other world," he says.

"Really?"

"The void is nothing but people's breath."

"So something survives?" I say.

"Feet survive. Feet and breath survive," he says,
"peoples' feet and peoples' breath."

"That is good news," I say.

"Don't mock me," he says.
"Do you know you still 'toe in'?
 That your head 'pitches forward'?
You're past the half-way mark, son.
God is not altruistic, you know,
He doesn't make exceptions.
Of course things are dark and light at once."

Huh? Who is he? Whoever was my father?

Bloodied in some Russian pogrom.
Nixon-lover on the North Side of Chicago.
Blue denim, bola tie Republican.

Rosicrucian cowboy in the Promised Land.

ARCH SUPPORTS—THE FITTING

Greets me in the waiting room,
father with waxed,
        five-eyelet shoes;
son, too, with spit-shine, five-eyelet shoes.
This is how I was brought up. I do it
        to show respect.
Value your feet.

"Okay, un-sock those feet of yours," he says,
"let's see the felons."
I unlace my Florsheims: moist feet emerging
from their cave of leather.
Father holds up arch supports.
Curved knife in hand, he shakes his head
        as he trims *just* so.

"Remind me. Why do I need these things?" I ask.
"Weak ankles and spine," he says. "Poor posture.
Your feet are fine.
Truth is, you should be more like your feet.
Robust, healthy feet.
Take a lesson from your feet," he says.

"Feet appreciate
        custom made.
No Dr. Scholl's for these feet."

Slips in the inserts.
Arch support like a shoe
inside a shoe,
leather inside leather.

"Every step I take you're going to be there," I say.
"Every step," he says, "every step of the way."

GOD IS IN THE CRACKS

"Just a tiny crack separates this world
from the next, and you step over it
        every day,
God is in the cracks."
Foot propped up, nurse hovering, phone ringing.
"Relax and breathe from your heels.
Now, that's breathing.
So, tell me, have you enrolled yet?"

"Enrolled?"

"In the Illinois College of Podiatry."

"Dad, I have a job. I teach."

"Ha! Well, I'm a man of the lower extremities."

"Dad, I'm fifty-three."

"So what? I'm eighty. I knew you
before you began wearing shoes.
Too good for feet?" he asks.
"*I. Me. Mind:*
        That's all I get from your poetry.
Your words lack feet. Forget the mind.
Mind is all over the place. There's no support.
You want me to be proud of you? Be a foot man.
Here, son," he says, handing me back my shoes,
"try walking in these.
Arch supports. Now there's a subject.
Some day you'll write about arch supports."

GOD'S PODIATRIST

Palm Springs, CA

Corns, calluses, pain
      in the joints of my toes.
Masked man in the half light,
starched white jacket and pants,
      shaking his head.
"Dad, what are you doing?"
"Re-fitting the supports.
What is it with you?" he asks,
"Why don't you respond?
I've never seen such feet.
With a word, the world came into being," he murmurs,
cigarette in hand.
"With you, with arch supports even
      there are these feet that go nowhere.
Anyway, there's just one person,
God, God's body," he says.
"God has a body?" I ask.
"Of course he has a body, and feet.
"Feet?"
"Feet, of course feet.
You know he's not one to ask for help."
      Throws me my shoes. "You're finished."
"Help?" I ask.
 "It's the least I can do," he says.
"You're a podiatrist for God?" I ask.
"Varicose veins.
The aroma of infinity.
feet sparking,   feet an endless ocean,
      feet made of music.
Of course I have to sort out foot from hallucination.
You can't treat a halo.
Don't look at me like that.
You're the one who doesn't respond to treatment.
God has feet like anyone else. You know it and I know it.
"I am that I am," I say.
"Says you," says my father.
"He is that he is and I'm his podiatrist.
What a son," he says.

Portrait of an L.A. Daughter

—The Family is the Country of the Heart.
— Guiseppe Massini, Italian Nationalist Leader

HANNAH

Her third eye is strawberry jam
has a little iris in it
her eyelids
      are red
she's sleepy
      and the milk
      has gone down
      the wrong way.
I've just had breakfast
with the smallest person in the world.

PORTRAIT OF AN L.A. DAUGHTER

Take #1

Braided blonde hair
white and pink barrettes
Bette Davis gorgeous
I hug her
dreamy daughter with no make-up
silver skull and crossbones
middle
      finger
          ring
three or four others in each ear
rings in her navel
rings on her thumbs
gentle moonchild
      "pal" she announces
to "Porno for Pyros"
formerly the group "Jane's Addiction"
 "Nothing's Shocking"
with Perry Farrell
Dave Navarro on guitar

and Stephen Perkins
on drums
Ain't No Right they sing.
"What are you,
          some kind of groupy?" I ask.
She says nothing.
          Just turns up the volume.
Been Caught Stealing
          they sing.

I hold her
Wet 'n' Wild lip gloss
diamond stud earrings
and glitter on her cheeks

Wan, she's looking wan
my dancing daughter

Hannah Davi –a new name–
walk-on in the movie *Day Of Atonement*
          with Christopher Walken

And a part in a Levitz Furniture ad
          ("it's work")
and a part in an MCI commercial
          ("Best Friends")
breaking in
Brotherhood Of Justice

a Swiss Alps bar-maid
("classic blonde Gretel")
in a Folger's Coffee commercial

"Grunge is in," she says
visiting Santa Cruz,
"any Goodwills around?"

                    *   *   *

Flashback

Appearing,
          "crowning" says the doctor

"Hannah" says her mother
"the name means 'grace'"

Two-year-old drooling
as I toss her into space
and back
        she falls
and back
into space again

Flawless teeth and perfect smile
one blue eye slightly larger than the other
her three-thousand miles away mother
still present as
two as one
two breathing together
we three breathe again as one
Hannah O Hannah

DANTE PARADISO, ACTRESS

White, eight-door, hot tub
        limo behind us   the driver
        on his horn

Move, dammit, move! he yells. No green light,
        no green arrow,
no green anything.

"I love L.A. traffic because it means
a whole lot of other people are here too."

She's half way into the intersection
waiting to make a left turn
                                against

Four lanes of oncoming DeVilles.
        "L.A.'s famous for this. I love
how huge it is," she says,

"seeing strangers I'll never see again. And the restaurants…
and the guys…

I should have been born here.
Anyway, I corrected the problem."

    Dante Paradiso,
          the original
Miss Fire Cracker. Youngest, Newest, Freshest
Ingénue.

Part in *Show Girls ("ugh!"),*
part—dancer—in *Forrest Gump.*

She is the sun and the moon.
Miss Gold Ring.

Applies *Crème d'Elegance.* "It tones the skin."
A little eyeliner,
         Maybelline *tres noir.*

"Look, look, there's Julia Roberts! See,
behind us."

Ms. Paradiso's the moon wearing make-up,
the sun reaching for blue eye-shadow,

     luminous,
         yellow, aqua beige and blue,

     the sky whitening,

turning, turning at last
pulling away from Ms. Roberts

     silicon limousine with a ready smile,

sunlight, sunlight, the Next Big Thing.

          —Los Angeles, 1999

TAKE ME HOME, I NEED REPAIR

Take me home, I need repair. Take me please to
anywhere.
                    —The Red Hot Chili Peppers

—*For my son, Nicholas*

He's a musician
            prophet
                        a raging Apollo
gold hoops,
            diamond stud earrings
toenails and fingernails
                        painted black

6'3", 200 pounds
legs propped up
on a wobbly stool

                    Listening
Magic-Red-Blood-Hot-Sugar
            Chili-Sex

What I see is insanity.
Whatever happened to humanity?

"Good lyrics," I say

"The Chili Peppers," he says
"it's rap and it sucks.
Actually, I like Punk more—"

White steel guitar in hand
he demonstrates:

Fuck you... he sings.
End of demonstration.

Now he's Anthony Keidis
a tube sock
        on his dick
One hot minute, and I'm in it...

Next he's trancey, anguished
Sonic Youth

Later:

Washing windows,
scrubbing floors,
        dancing
doing
        standup
                impressions

My son the genie
my son Mr. Clean

Tries to jump into my arms.
Where do kids come from anyway?

                "Fucking life
                Everything sucks," he says

Mourning Kurt Cobain,
        Hillel Slovak and the others
overdose dead.

Youthanasia

Whip-smart

Funk Da World
Funk Da World

I'm the father, I'm supposed to tell him—what?

"I know the truth," he says,
"I know the truth."

WATER BREATHER: FOUR FOR MICHAEL

1. SWIMMER IN AIR

Gulper of sea,
swimmer in air,

he dives, dives in again
again
      water's
           water,
air is air.

"Water's
      water,
air is air,"
      I say.
"No," he says, "no."

He's the breather of water,
three-year-old refuser,
         won't be taught.

Intent, he makes his run,
big feet slapping, loopy leap
and sinks
      to the bottom.

Swim to him.

"Water's
      water," I begin...
he's red-eyed, sputtering, shaking—
Clambers up the ladder
         to the dock
           and jumps.

Scoop and hug him close
      hold him out.

"Stroke, stroke
                    inhale
                              in air
exhale in water," I say,
                    "like this, Michael."
"Breathe in air,
                    swim in water."

"No," he says, "no."

Slap, slap,   his feet
on the side of the dock

He breathes in water
and swims in the air

breathes in water
and swims in air.

2. JULY 4

*A boy achieves maximum pissing power
at age 5 or 6....*
                              —Dr. Ed Jackson

"Michael, what the—"

six-year-old, dick in hand,
turning, his stream unbroken,

nine feet if it's an inch,
          laughing, the kid's laughing
as he circles

360-degrees
hand all the time on the throttle,
slowly, back arched

he stands
          "Dick, dink, decker,
                    weener, peter, pecker..." he sings
crowd gathering

nine feet from VW rooftop
to raging Mr. Beer-In-His-Hand.
"Is that your kid up there?"

I should laugh,
        get up there with him,
lead our friends in applause.

        "Dick, dink, decker," he sings,
face shining, joy to the world.

Rein him in, *do something,*
Jesus K. Christ,

"Dance," I want to say, "dance
on the roof of the German machine.

"Piss on, piss all you want—
What a stream!" I want to say.

Old fool, old scold,
too fearful to sing
"O Stream of Gold…"

Fucked father, fucked-up father,
I spank him instead.

3. HOUSE BOAT

Lasqueti Island, B.C.

Washing dishes in the darkness
with a hose,
I spray off the few
        remnants
of spaghetti onto the oysters

In their beds below.   _
Inside the single room
there is no running water—
        only the green hose
on the deck of our floating home.

We secure the lines,
bathe and sing, *We all live in a Yellow Submarine...*
I reach out in the darkness
hearing my son brushing his teeth
to borrow his toothbrush.

I cannot find my own:
Tasting
          my fourteen-year-old son's
mouth inside my mouth.
Then we find more dishes

And, as the moon rises and the lines
          go tight,
continue scrubbing and drying silverware
and plates,
          two dishwashers reading Braille.

4. **MOUNTAIN SOLITAIRE**

i. Jerome, Arizona

He's thirty-two, my age
when he was born.
Haven't seen him for four years,
estranged son of estranged wife.

Phone:
          "Please... leave... message..."
                    says the machine.
"Hey, Michael... It's Dad!"
He won't pick up, won't call back.

I court him, send gifts:
          "Oh, boy, a cordless phone
from, let's see now, Mr. Walk-around...
my much-doodling daddy!"

I see him shake his head.
And write, I write him a poem.
Read it onto his answering machine.

"Dick, dink, decker,
    weener, peter, pecker..."

He's away—a girlfriend
plays back the message.
"There's a stalker..." she tells him.
"No, that's my father," he says,
and calls me. He likes the poem.

ii. *Golden Gate Park*

We meet and he leads me
to the Hall of Flowers,
his dark hair combed forward,
bushing out over his ears,
        single white strand glinting in the sun.

He's three, six and thirty-two;
I'm thirty-two, thirty-eight and sixty-four.
The prodigal father
        and the abandoned 'live alone,'
Mr. Mountain Solitaire.

We stroll through the Garden of Fragrance,
oasis of lakes.
            Absentee father
fathering,

he the fathered, fatherless
hungering

        son to be a father
        father to be father

This is the hunger.

            —San Francisco, 1998

SEX & TV WITH AUNT MIRIAM — 1945

Part 1

"Always wash your hands after you've played in the backyard with those leaves and things before touching yourself," said my aunt, beginning our affair with this public service announcement.

"Yes, ma'am."

"Bobby, I'm going to show you how broadminded I am."

"Okay."

"But first I want you to tell me what you do with Lenore and her sister."

"Nuthin."

"You spin the bottle?"

"Yeah."

Luminous brown-eyed English Miriam abuzz with heat,
My left arm around her, my right hand
in her right hand
      "Kiss me   love me   feel me, Bobby…"

I'm a pleaser. But… what was it she wanted me to do?

                              A seventh grader, I'd been held
back a year at school. "He tries hard, and he's smart about some things, but…" Anyway, I was right in there for a while with the slow learners.

Four thousand feet down in a North of England coal mine,
I'd just have grabbed a shovel and gotten to work.
I'd have known right away what to do.

Holding me with one hand,
marking with the other,
D-I-C-K, wrote my twenty-something aunt.
Hmm. It felt good.

She finished by drawing some arrows and a bull's eye on her own body.

What was it like? It was like television, "informative and entertaining."
Never to have been fucked and never to have watched television either,
and then to be fucking and watching the evening news
on one of the first TVs in Chicago, and the Atomic
Bomb going off and the war over all at the same time, I think...
the truth is, I still don't understand.

The diagrams and the lettering helped.
I like seeing things labeled.
I'm so grateful.

"All art aspires to the state of music." That's true. I know that. And even
at thirteen I loved Gershwin (*Rhapsody in Blue*), but I knew *real* music
when I heard it. "O do me, thrill me." And *that's* what I went for. *That's*
what I learned at thirteen. And *that's* what I'm grateful for.

O Miriam, say it again. Tell me where you want it. Draw me a picture.
Ah, dearest, how helpful it's been having those letters printed on my
dick.

                    How many times have I been told,
"Bobby, you don't know your ass from a hole in the ground"? More
times than there are stars in the sky. And I hold my head high. At least I
know where, O Aunt Miriam, O Miriam, to look for my dick.

*   *   *

Part 2

Fifty-two years later

"Oh, my God! I can't stand it," she said, hearing my voice.
"How *are* you, Bobby? I've been trying to find you. You're
a missing person, you know?"

"I write, I've even published," I said.

"I talked to that publisher of yours. Famous you're not."

"I know, I know. And what about you, Miriam?"

"I got some health problems. I go to temple, the *B'nai Brith.*"

"And Uncle Jerry?"

"Dead. That's why I'm calling, Bobby. He's dead. Fifty-four years we'd been together." Uncle Jerry, the handsomest man in Chicago, circa 1945, singer on Chicago's WGN Radio.

"No one thought it would work. Fifty-four years and we yelled all the time. What does anyone know about anything?"

"You stuck it out," I say. "That's good."

> She's twenty-one, twenty-two,
> pale, pinkie-brown where I put my lips.
>
> "Enjoy yourself, Bobby. Life is to enjoy."
> "What about Jerry? What about Uncle Jerry?"
>
> "Listen to me. People go up and back between loving
>   and not loving.
> Do you understand, Bobby?"
>
> My lips here, there...
> She's teaching me. "This is how you do it."
>
> "See," she says, "see."
> I'm thirteen and not wanting to. Then
> wanting.
>
> "I want to."

Woof, woof.

"That's Koko. That dog has a weight problem.
"She doesn't want to move
"so I let her sleep on our bed.
"Koko is on morphine."

"Your dog is on morphine?"

"Did you ever hear of such a thing?
"Listen, you're all I got, Bobby.
"you're all the family that's left."

She wants me to fly to Chicago to see her.
"Do I have to draw you a picture?

"Come, Bobby. Come and see the sights."

We lie together... Betty Grable mouth
and red red lipstick
watching some old movie.
Listening at the same time to the radio.
It's the second half of a doubleheader.
Cubs versus the Pirates.
and the Cubs are ahead 4-3.

"That's good, Bobby. That's good.
"It's The Star Spangled Banner,
"O God, don't stop,
"It's The Stars and Stripes Forever.
"The Battle Hymn of the Republic.
"God Save the Queen!
"Do you understand?
"Don't stop."

She's pushing eighty, she says, and sells Avon. "It's a living."

I'm grateful, I want to say. I'm grateful for the arrows.
Whatever else has changed, I will always remember.

The aurora borealis,
and dawn's early light.
That was the year the Cubs won the pennant.

I understand, Miriam, these are the ties that bind.
Broad stripes and bright stars.
America the beautiful.
Purple mountains and spacious skies,
the screwed and sweetly screwy,
this our family, and this our country,

sweet land of liberty,
O fruited plain, O amber fields of grain,
from your apartment house to ours
('til Mom found out)
of thee, O darling, of thee I sing.

DICK IN THE DRAWER

What his dick was doing
in that dresser drawer
I have no idea,

Mom and Dad
         getting dressed or undressed,

she must have closed it
just shut it *bang!* without looking,

"Dammit!"
            "O my God! O no!"

his *schlong*
         half in,
                  half out

of that bonnet top highboy,
wedding gift from Grandpa.

This time he doesn't whack her or get angry.

"I'll bandage it," she offers.

Ten year old in the next room,
I hear what I hear

"No," he says, his voice softening,
and again she offers,

"Filet of sole," she whispers, "jelly roll,
shimmy up the Maypole.

"Flag pole, peep hole…"
something about a camisole.

Home again, whole again

Mom and Dad again,
back in bed again.

MILLIONAIRE

—Grandpa Max, 1860-1958

1. His inventions

Born in 1860, Austro-Hungarian immigrant,
inventor of a cap to keep the fizz
in seltzer bottles, a refinement to the machine gun,
and a metal Rube Goldberg bookmark
        sold with a diagram and user manual,
Grandpa made big money speculating,
buying and selling tenements.
In the 1920s, offered stock in a start-up selling
flavored water and cocaine, he turned it down. "Coca Cola," he spat.
"Vhat dreck! Who'd buy?"

2. His economies

Lean, stiff-necked, pack-a-day smoker
with a fondness for syrupy wine, he wouldn't own a car,
used public transportation;
and, rather than buy toilet paper,
blackened his ass with yesterday's *Chicago Tribune.*

Grandpa never left a restaurant
—"vegetable soup, roll, glass of water"—
without pocketing a few cellophane-wrapped crackers
        "for later."

At six, I got my first lesson in thrift.
Grandpa with a smoker's cough:
"Cough into four corners of hanky,
like this—
four coughs minimum—,
before you dirty up the middle."
End of lesson.

3. His curses

Late summer afternoons, partaking of Mogen David
("Shield of David") wine,
he orbited the living room, sonofabitching
the government
                    and Democrats with no sense,
Franklin and Eleanor Roosevelt, "betrayers of the rich,
and they stole my patent, too."

God damning union leaders, *schnorrers,*
the United Mine Workers,
the AFL and CIO,
"Stand 'em up against a wall.
Shoot 'em, shoot the sons-a-bitches."

4. His secret to health and long life

Old Testament Moses,
cigarette and drink in hand,
white mustache, gray beard, pacing, pacing,
"God" (it was a prayer after all),
"damn" (the patriarch calling down wrath),
"son-a-bitch, son-a-bitch."
The last of his great inventions,
five syllables to God's four ("Let there be light"),
but good enough.
And that is how he'd breathe, cursing
—head back, chin up—everyone who, he figured,
had somehow cost him money.
"God damn son-a-bitch, God damn son-a-bitch!" he'd rage,
miraculously cured of whatever ailed him.

THE BIGGEST PARTY ANIMAL OF THEM ALL

The biggest party animal of them all
spoke Hindi, a little English,
suffered from diabetes,
                    was allergic to incense,
flowers and perfume,

loved chocolate,
>gave it away, used it as *prasad,*
a gift to his disciples.

In his 70s he gave himself away,
reportedly 'poking' as many as 300
of his youngest followers.

'Now's your chance,' he'd say, his mouth full.
'That's right, child. Lie back,
meditate,' he'd croon. 'Have faith.'

The dude separated so many people from so much money
he had to create the Guru Om Foundation.
Rolls Royces, chauffeurs, ashrams in all the major cities.

The movement started small, twenty,
>thirty,
>>then hundreds,
>>>soon—
>doctors, lawyers,
hoteliers, cocaine dealers and professors,
>>dancers, artists
>and musicians
flocked to him,
himself a musician, masked actor, comic,
>storyteller
>>extraordinaire.
>>>Flatulent, potbellied old mystic,
giver-away of toys, party hats and favors to devotees.
The 'hundred-hatted yogi' we called him.

God, he was fun to be around!

Festivals with world-renowned performers,
dinner for five thousand,
>>and, afterwards,
we got to approach and touch his feet.

True, sometimes he'd flip out, become enraged,
have to be strapped down
or held,
>one devotee at each limb.
Rudra the Howler.

Then, reviving,
'Chant.' 'Dance.' 'Meditate.'
Nataraj, the dancing Shiva, O graceful one!

Once, mid-revelry, irked by something I'd read aloud,
he drew back, swatted me four, five times
with a mass of peacock feathers. *Whoosh! Whoosh!*

It's known as *Shaktipat,* kick-start Kundalini yoga,
where the party thrower has only to touch someone—
blow to the head or soft caress—

and Zap!

For two, maybe three, minutes
I saw two worlds interpenetrating

jewels into jewels,
silver suns, electric whiteness,

World 'A' and world 'B'
one vibrating blue pearl,

world like a skyful of blue suns
Whoosh! Whoosh! Whoosh!

Head spinning, I began to laugh,
and he too, old cobra face,
          began to howl,

mister three in one. Mister one in three.

O thou paunchy one
          in Birkenstocks
                    and orange silk robe, trickster,
magician,
          master cocksman,
hit me again!

Seven years I hung out with him,
even flew to India, meditated
                    in his cave

chanting to
      scorpions, malaria mosquitoes
so illumined they chanted back.

        phallic god,
        god in the shape of a dick,
            godfather
            con man

        killer god, god of death
        and destroyer of all life

        'Sonofabitch,' I say
        'Sonofabitch!'
        The guests are still arriving,
        the party's just begun.

                —*Oakland, California*

FASHION MAKES THE HEART GROW FONDER

      Marriage and hanging go by destiny.
        —Robert Burton, *Anatomy of Melancholy*

Partygoers
Her fruity, floral fragrance—
Honey at her dressing table
      like a pilot in the cockpit,
a woman armed with old *TV Guides,* catalogs,
ordering information
      for all the major scents and potions.

She put on (how can I describe them?)
refrigerator avocado green
      and white
Keith Partridge bell bottoms. Incandescent,
no less bizarre, I wore purple velveteen pants
and a tie-dyed shirt.

Her old lover Warren was there in his pimp suit,
      giant bug-eye sunglasses
and huge fake fur pimp hat,
a party with vintage Joan Crawford movies,

Honey wearing Chanel No. 5,
        the first synthetic scent.

And me, her consort, I wore
'a blend of crisp citrus and warm spice, mossy woods, a scent
for the feeling man.'

I remember her silver and turquoise earrings
on the make-up table
as the bed jumped and jerked
those first two years.

Ravi Shankar, Thai weed, and a little homegrown,
that velvet ribbon choker with butterflies
and the scent of Honey when she dropped her
        tooled leather belt on the floor.

Then, "Tell me what you want," I said.
"You can't give me what I want."
"What do you want?"
"I'm out of style and so are you.
I want to lose weight."

And like that it was over.

"How about this handbag?" offered *Cosmo,*
"the perfect accessory
to the outfit you wear
when you leave your husband."

And that's how it ended. Honey at some fashion show
throwing back her head, the spotlight playing
on her face and neck.

Yes, I could see what Honey wanted,
to shop where she'd never shopped before,
to pull on high leather boots
and a mini-skirt; then, beaded Navaho handbag in hand,
flashing a little scented thigh, walking out on someone
who couldn't keep up,
a jerk in tie-dye.

I loved the woman, longed to stay with her and,
to do so, if I could have, arm-in-arm with her,
I'd have walked out on myself.

POST-MODERN—A (MOSTLY) FOUND POEM*

"Joan of Arc was married to the Biblical Noah."
"The inhabitants of Egypt were called mummies,
and built pyramids in the shape of triangular cubes."

"The Pyramids are a range of mountains between France
and Switzerland."

He graded his papers
    and went home to Honey.

"Areas of the dessert are cultivated by irritation."

Honey and the teacher were newlyweds.
Filing her nails, she watched some Joan Crawford movie.
Handed him a joint.

"Get your papers graded?" Applying nail polish,
Honey reached for *Cosmopolitan*,
turned back to the *TV Guide*.

All pink and red she was
and full of self-esteem and bounce,
teacher's fluorescent bride.

"Now or never," Honey said, her eyes twinkling,

"Post-civilization, post-modern, post-Cracker Jack,
early unforeseeable, post paradigm.

"Now you see it, now you don't."

"They lived in the Sarah Dessert and traveled by Camelot."

"In the dessert, the climate is such
the inhabitants have to live elsewhere."

"Come and get it," Honey called.
"Come and get it."

"In Europe, the enlightenment was a reasonable time."

———

*With thanks to Richard Lederer's *Fractured English*

MY MUSE

> *As a rule, the power of absolutely falling in love soon van-*
> *ishes... because the woman feels embarrassed by the spell*
> *she exercises over her poet-lover and repudiates it...*
> —Robert Graves, *The White Goddess*

"Why don't you just write a poem, right now?" she says.
'Western wind, when wilt thou blow...'
why don't you write a poem like that,
like that 'Anonymous'? Something inspirational."

"Talk about muses," I sulk,
"Yeats' wife was visited in her dreams by angels
saying, 'We have come to bring you images
for your husband's poetry.'"

"Yeah? So what?" she says. "It's out of style.
I already do too much for you."

Odalisque in a wicker chair,
book open on her lap,
dry Chardonnay at her side,
hand on a dozing, whiskered Sphinx.

"You need a muse," she says, "someone beautiful, mysterious,
some long-lost love,
        fragile, a dancer perhaps. Look at me..."

"Yeah?" I say, refilling her glass,
"You hear me complaining? You're *zaftig*."
        "Zaftig?"
    "Firm, earthy, juicy, too," I say.

            *   *   *

"Juicy plum," I say, in bed, left hand over her head,
"rose petals," I say, right arm around her.
"Silver drop earrings," I murmur, ordering out
for gifts. "Aubergine scarf, gray cashmere cardigan."

I do this in my sleep. Go shopping in my sleep.
"Oh, yeah, and a case of Chardonnay."
Wake to the scent of apple blossoms,
decades in the glow of rose light.

                  *   *   *

"Wake," she whispers. I tell her my dream.
We kiss. Poppy Express. Racy Red. Red Coral.
            Star Red.
                        Red red.

"Enough. That's enough," she says.

AMNESIA

Somewhere an ocean of doorknobs,
a cemetery for seaweed.

                        The sailors,
                  all of them,
            walking
      at
some slight angle
counter to the angle
everyone else
walks at.
The ships and the rain
 slanting
   at still
      another
         angle.
And music
and the woman
one has children by
bears her child
and her belly
every day
at a different
angle.

We are under water
Come up and the surf is filled with rooftops, planes overhead
narrowly missing trees, it begins raining upwards.

Things get lonely to go outside.
Sometimes the body gets lonely to go outside.
Sometimes everything and the body also goes outside
                    at once.

Every morning at precisely that moment
the woman asks for his dreams,
he has none,
or forgets or wants to forget or
conceives he is dying.
In his memory
they break up
almost entirely
because he can not
remember his dreams.
On the other hand, she remembers hers
and tells them
compulsively.

He reads bed sheets. Imprint of lines. The woman's neck.
The word "Mother" tattooed somewhere. A cluster of red
freckles above the "M." She sits up and yawns.
"I want," she says, "I want."

THE WAY TO JACK'S HOUSE

> *Foley's a deepener, he gives substance*
> *to issues under view.*
> > —Michael McClure.

Santa Cruz to Oakland

"I have an appointment with light,"
        said Anthony Holdsworth
arriving to paint Jack's portrait.
I too have an appointment,
but, listening—Foley on cassette—

multiculturalism...
many fibers, each qualifying the other,
each creating a condition of
'hidden relevancies...'

I make a wrong turn,
        Hegenberger
instead of Alameda,
           miss the Coliseum,
miss High, then Fruitvale...

Pay the toll, cross the Oakland Bay Bridge,
return via Treasure Island.

    'Double' and 'doubt,' 'double' and 'doubt.'
    To 'doubt' something is to think 'two' ways
    about it.

"Look at you, you have no sense of direction,
your mind—what you call your mind—
is a cacophony of voices," says one of those voices.
"Truth is, there's no there there,
and there's no here here either."

How to proceed? I'm fucking lost.
    Moment of panic.
Old two-door Honda pushing 65,
        everyone else going 80.
Surviving is surviving to see my friend.
All I want in life by now
        is to see my friend.

    'Individual' means 'not divided.'
    I'm divided, but it's a good thing.

I'm divided too, but I'm not sure
        it's a good thing.

I head south past the Coast Guard Station,
past Broadway, Lake Merritt in the rear view mirror,
the Hall of Justice, the Oakland Museum,
        14th Avenue, 22nd...

Ten minutes from Jack's house
I ease in a new tape—

> *O what a, O water; the hum*
> *of multitudes, the home of multitudes,*
> *the hymn, the ham, the him*
> *of multitudes...*

Here's Fruitvale again,
here's High.
Make the turn, make another.
There it is, stucco and brick
on a quiet corner,
bird of paradise,
orange poppies
        Jack on the doorstep,
his dark-rimmed glasses
and the longish hair,
"eyes full of interest,
some inward thing made manifest,"
        (his words, his words
                        and my words) friend.
"A bright passageway,
a haven for light,"
        he calls Oakland,
"a haven for me."

"So how was the trip?" he asks.

"No problem, Jack. No problem at all."

THE HOUSE ON STILTS

Cross Lake, Wisconsin - Illinois 1950

There is no sleep, this night
in me, in the room
where I write my sleep.
I open the window, and unhook
the screen; the bushes, metal lawn chairs
        streetlamps
the moon, pieces of a livingroom.

Stilts, rotted long pilings,
stand just beneath the bookcase, TV,
bedroom and kitchen,
the four corners of the house.

         The sky,
a starry imitation ceiling–
our family, propped,
         house-on-stilts people,
goiter, bulgy-eyed mother,
         weekend father,
half in one state, half in
another
                    dots and dashes on the map,
Cross Lake with a line
running through it.

               *   *   *

The highway alive, aloud
a blatant strip of rug.
         And people,
         in their houses,
         the back doors opening, slamming.

         Every hour
someone screams quietly for a while.
And babies, in little closed windows.
The TV, a bluish, fluorescent hearth.

–Tilting, facing
         its double, the house on stilts.

A house in the shape, a dream
         in the shape, of itself
         of its house, of its dream.

         A sleep
the impossibility of sleep,
the vision, the life that it requires.
Her eyes opening, singing,
my mother, former Miss Chicago,
         on a springboard.

PRAYER FOR MY MOTHER

May the Great Name be blessed...

1. Mother's Limousines

"Mourn like a Jew," Grandfather says,
tearing my shirt
           from the collar down,
"and when she's buried, rip out the grass
      and wail.
Expose your heart. Lament for her."

        Mother, mother
        mother of the inflamed heart.

Car door slamming behind us as we exit...

Bar-mitzvah'd boy, 13, I say it once,
say what I'm told to say,
"He is the Rock, His work is perfect..."
Say it,
        YIT-GA-DAL
        V'YIT-KA-DASH
        SH'MEI
        RA-BA
        B'AL MA...
    the Kaddish of sounds, not words

"May a great peace from heaven..." I say,
"May His great Name be blessed,
...Magnified and sanctified...
        Y'HAY
        SH'LAMA
        RA-BA
        MIN SH'MAYA
        V'CHAYIM
        ALENU... I say.

...a week later,
        no to the rabbi,
        no to morning,
        no to twilight,
           no to the mid-day prayer
no repeating the prayer three times a day for a year
        no, I say, and no to the *shul.*

           "We're animals first and human second,
           and there is no God. Do you hear me?"

Fox-trotting mother. Dancer mother. Beauty Queen.
        in the house of prayer.

           "Mom," I ask, "how do you pray?"
           She shakes her head and turns away.
                "Snap out of it," she says.

           "Better to go shopping," she says,
           "better to get a job, better to make money."
           I reach out. "Mom—"

           "Hands off," she says, **"hands off."**

           "Kids," she says. ***"Oi vay."***
               "Holocaust," she says. ***"Oi, oi, oi."***
                  "God," she says.
                      "What God?"

"Bless the Lord who is blessed," I don't pray.
"May the Great Name be blessed," I don't pray,
        but burn a candle so Mother,
Miss Chicago,
           can find her way back.

           Later, I cannot recall her face.
           "...you're not to look on any photo of her,
                not for seven days," says Grandfather.
           What did she even look like?
           Faceless son
                mourning a faceless mother,
                mourning her,

                mourning
                        freelance,
                mourning on the fly.

"She'll wander for seven days," Grandfather says,
"then, when she's wormed, her soul will return to God."

                        lacks a body and I can't recall her face
                        lacks a body and I can't recall her face

"Save her soul from Gehenna.
"Join us," pleads the rabbi.
                No, no is my prayer
No to duty and no to prayer.

Who was she? Some brunette rich girl
I never knew,
        a stranger dead at 42.
Mother, the beautiful secretary.
I touch her in a dream. She turns,
and there's no one there.

I shake from head to foot.
I stand and I sway.
"Mother, Mother," I say.

Blessed be the stranger.
No, no to the stranger,
no to the stranger.

No is my Kaddish.
No is my prayer.
I am the no
I am the not.

I will not be her savior,
I will not.

2. Gehenna, or Purgatory

                Mother applies Pond's Beauty Cream. Her face glistens.
                Massages her forehead with one hand,
                holds the other to her heart.

"What's the point?" she asks, cigarette ablaze,
mouth tightening.

When she dies, they bury her not in a shroud,
but in pancake make-up
and best gray dress.

"Turn the photos to the wall," says Grandfather,
"and cover your lips.
That's right. Now cover your face.
Isolate yourself — groan — let your hair grow wild.
The mourner is the one without a skin, says the Talmud.
Understand? You are no longer whole."
And I think: *I am going to die, too.*

Sit in silence and say nothing.

"How about a prayer to locusts?" I pray,
"How about a prayer to boils?

"O murdering heaven," I pray.

Grandfather cooks lentils,
lentils and eggs. "Mourners' food," he calls it.

*"A prayer to rats,
and a prayer to roaches."*

"Death is the mother of beauty," he says.
"The death of another makes you want to die," he says.
"The Angel of Death is made entirely of eyes," Grandfather says.

Damn seeing,
Damn touching.
Damn feeling.
Damn loving.

In Jewish hell—

I am the unknowing,
the not Jewish Jew.

Split, cloven,
	cracked

      In hell

      nameless,
      and eyeless,
          faceless.
      No, no to blessings,
      no to teachings,
      no to reading from right to left.

      I pray with them,
      I pray with the no, I pray with the not.
      I pray with the dead, I pray with the damned.

      God, God who is a wound, we pray.

3. Against Darkness

      "Kaddish is a song against darkness," says the rabbi.
      YIT-GA-DAL
      V'YIT-KA-DASH
      SH'MEI
      RA-BA
      B'AL MA...
          "'Magnified and sanctified
            May His Great Name Be...'
      No it says, no to darkness. No to nothingness.
         'May His Great Name be blessed.'
      Kaddish praises God...
      Kaddish: a mourner's prayer
      that never mentions death.
      Y'HAY
      SH'LAMA
      RA-BA
      MIN SH'MAYA
      V'CHAYIM...

"Now then, Let R__, the son of G__,
      come forward," says the rabbi,
but I freeze, pretend not to hear.

Again he calls, calls me to say Kaddish.
(Loudly) "Let R__, son of G__, step beside me."
Ten other mourners turn in my direction.

Again I pretend not to hear.
Staring, face crimson, then white, he turns
        and continues with the service.

                The Lord is our God, the Lord is One...
                I mourn her — mourn Kaddish — mourn *shul*
                and head for home. Age 13, I walk out
                      looking
                              for stones
                I might hurl into heaven.

            *   *   *

                I am the un-*bar'd mitzvah*,
                escaped
                      Jew from nowhere,
              apostate,
              skipped Jew,
                    cleft Jew,
         Jew, pause in the beating of the heart.

            *   *   *

                Once home, I pray, "Damn Him,
                    "damn G-d," I pray.

            *   *   *

Mother, car door slamming,
        the shovel biting
Mother, whose body is the world,
        spinning into space—

"Life rattles," she says.
"My son, His Royal Highness," she says,
        "get used to it."

"Mom, is there an afterlife?"
"Shape up," she says. **"You are my afterlife.**
        God help us."

4. Anniversary

"We're just subdivisions of one person.
One's no better than any other.
Someone dies and you move forward
      into the front lines," Grandfather says,
         lighting a *yortzeit* candle.

            "'Blessed art thou who raises the dead...'"

Shaking the match, he turns. *"Gottenyu!"* he says.
"I should have been next."
Tears well up
      and I see him see her
           in me.

"Same color hair,
      same eyes..." Grandfather says.
 "Remember seeing her in her coffin?" he asks,
      grabbing my arm.
"Your mother didn't believe, but she'll be raised
and rest with G-d. Does love quit?

"Can you feel her... hear her inside you?"
I nod.
"Where?"
"Here, in my chest."
"And what does she say?"
"She says nothing," I reply,
      but she does:
           "Loopy doop," she says, *"Rest in peace!*
           Wait'll you die, you'll see. There is no peace.
           When you're dead,
                you're dead.
         Enough.
      Meshugge!" she says, and shakes her head.

"Pray, damn you," he says. "It's your mother."

"…Now it's over," he sobs.
        "But you, the un-mourner
will mourn for her all your life.

"Jew, Jew without beginning," he mocks,
"Jew who got away,
        sinner, sinner," he yells,
"snap out of it."

Heavenly Sex, 2002

SON OF THE COMMANDMENT

Chicago

"So, twelve years old! Soon you'll be *bar mitzvah,*
          a *mensch,* a human being. Yes,
a human being, you. 'Today I am a man,' you'll say.
Let's see what you know:
The serpent in the Bible, what language does he speak?

"What's wrong with you? He speaks Hebrew. Same as God.
Same as Abraham and Isaac.
Same as Jesus.
Who else speaks Hebrew?

"Adam and Eve. Noah, too, and the animals:
the giraffe, the kangaroo, the lion.
          Hebrew.
                    Hebrew.
Soon you'll speak Hebrew.
Yes, and you'll read it too. *Apostate!*

"You're going to Hebrew School.

"Why? So you can speak to God in His own language.
Lesson One: *Bar* means son, *mitzvah* means commandment.
Bar mitzvah: Son of the commandment.
Commandment, *mitzvah:* What God gave to Moses.

"Lesson Two: When did Jews get souls?

"Souls they got when they got *Torah.*
Torah. Torah is Commandments.
Torah is soul.

"So learn, *bar mitzvah* boy! Read. Learn the blessing.
Do it right and you'll see
          the letters fly up to heaven.

"Learn. Yes. There's money
          in puberty,

money in learning. Books, money, fountain
pens... Always remember: learning is the best merchandise.

"Lesson Three: *Daven* means pray. You rock back and forth
like the rabbi,
and pray. In Hebrew.
From your mouth to God's ear.
But it has to be in Hebrew.
And you can't mispronounce:
And no vowels to make it easy."

WHAT WAS GOD THINKING?

1. At the Hospital

Father:
"I don't understand. What was God thinking,
what was He thinking?"

> *Mother:*
> *What's to understand?*
> *I'm dead.*
> *We weren't made to last.*
> *What's to understand?*
> *Ach, he doesn't hear me.*

Father:
"God forgive me.
A good woman. At least may she rest in peace."

> *Mother:*
> *Rest in peace? I'm dead for god sake.*
> *What good will rest do?*
> *You rest in peace.*
> *And something else, my friend, no viewing,*
> *no 'open casket.' They want to look at me, let them*
> *go look at someone else. Later,*
> *if they want to visit, fine.*
> *They know the address.*

But no flowers. Tell them. No flowers.
 Flowers die.
Stones they should bring, not flowers.
And as for afterlife, tell them, there is no 'afterlife.'
Look at him. He doesn't hear a word I'm saying.

2. The End of the World

Father:
"He stripped your mother, son,
 stripped the soul from her body.
You think a human life is not a world?
So then mourn,
 mourn for the end of the world.
And cover the mirrors.
Oi, look at you:
 Take off those shoes.
This is not a time for leather.
Here, let me tear that shirt for you.
Why? Because your mother's dead. God did her in;
her death should cost you something too.
That's right and put ashes on your head.
You're sitting *shiva* now.
 It's the law. You're a Jew.
Read the small print.
Seven days you cannot leave the house.
No radio, no TV, no looking at magazines,
 no books.
You'll see what death is like.
She's gone, so mourn, damn you, mourn!"

AFTER THE FUNERAL

At the Rosicrucian Altar

Sweeps away incense and candles,
 liquid-filled crystal flask...
"Forget prayer, forget everything I ever said."
Bolts the door, pours himself a drink.

Said about what, dad?

"What? Prayer. *Everything*. Forget it!
God doesn't need your prayer.
Now put on your shoes and get out of here."

> But dad, this stuff is just beginning
> to make sense.

"Nonsense," he says.

> What about the unseen?

"Goddammit, if it isn't seen,
it isn't there.
She's dead. Your mother's dead.
What are you, stupid?"
Reaches for matches. Lights a cigarette.

> But what about... soul?

"Soul? You know better than that.
There is no soul."

> And the 'other side'?

"There is no other side. You want to know
what's on the other side? Nothing.
That's what's on the other side.
Ach, you're looking for meaning.
>   Meaning's on backorder.
The sun and the moon and the stars,
>   They're all on backorder.
Nothing's there. Nothing ever existed.
>   She's dead. Don't you get it? The world is just a word.
Talmud says.
>   *Earth is a flaming word.*
That's it. That's it. End of story."

THE ROSICRUCIAN ONE DOLLAR BILL

"Franklin was a Rosicrucian.
He made it. He made
            the one dollar bill.
Open your wallet, take out a dollar.
Money talks, in pictures
            it talks. See,
                        Egyptian pyramid.
Money, American money
            with a pyramid.
The eagle, that you understand,
            thunderbolts in one hand,
olive branch in the other.
So, the pyramid,
            what does *that* say?
'You have no idea,' it says,
'you don't know the value of money.
Money is to remind you
what's important in life.' Look:
see, a halo with lines...
            above the pyramid,
'Glory,' that's what they call it,
a 'Glory,' burst of light
with the eye of God inside.
But the pyramid is unfinished, it needs work, like you.

"'*Ach,* enough! Enough with money,' says money.
Just remember, God has His eye on you.
And the sun and the moon and the stars are inside you.
So listen, listen to the pyramid.
You can't buy your way into heaven, it's true,
but you need to know money to get there."

LENORE AND THE LEOPARD DOG—FOUR POEMS

[Mother dies and father's heart attacks him.]

1. Catahoula Leopard Dog

Lenore K. appears at our door.
Father greets her. He wears
    a silk bathrobe,
big horn rimmed glasses
and his eyes bob up and down;
"I'm feeling better…"

        You better be better.

Lenore shakes out her shoulder-length,
    silvery-blond hair.
Poppa's eyes widen. Heart attack or no heart attack,
he's ready. Already he's ready.

LOOK, ALREADY HE'S READY, says Leopard Dog,
racing room to room, one brown eye,
one blue eye, sizing me up.
LIKE IT OR NOT, SONNY, WE'RE HERE TO STAY.

        Oh, why, hello there, little boy.
        I'm Daddy's new friend.

        And that, that meshugge
        is a Catahoula Leopard Dog… see the spots?
        And smart. He understands everything.

"A handsome wife develops the mind of man," Father says.

"No, please, dad," I whisper, "I don't want her,
I don't want another mother."

        He cups my face
      in his hand.
"Goddammit, I've told you, it's not good
for a man to be alone. And a little boy
needs a mother."

Leopard dog wags his tail. *WOOF, WOOF.* Stands
on his hind legs, paws on my shoulders.

WE'RE MOVING IN, *VERSTEHST?*
Springs across the room, switches on
     I Love Lucy.

Lenore sets the table.

> *What a dog! He just loves television. Mmm...*
> *that Ricky Ricardo, look at those yummy*
> *bedroom eyes.*

Shh, says Father.

> *You told me yourself, God is right there*
> *in the pleasure. O, you're good, doctor,*
> *you're good,* she whispers.

2. The Mystery of the Mouth

Later that night

"Your breasts are like twins, young roes
which feed
     among the lilies."

Leopard Dog and I listen at the door.

> *What are you talking about, honey?*

AH, HERE COME THE BIRDS AND BEES, says Dog.

"It's in the Bible. A woman's breasts
are the Ten Commandments, the two tablets
of God's law. One for what God allows,
     one for what He doesn't."

> *Talk sense. You're a doctor,* she laughs.

I peek through the keyhole.

Father's kneeling by the bed, pouring wine.

> *What about kissing?*

"Kissing is praying too, darling. Look, I bow my head,
same as when I pray."

"They make me sick," I say.

"I've told you before, dear, God rewards you for kissing."

Lenore sits up in bed. *Whaa—?*

"The way we make love is the way God will be with us.
With the mouth alone it is possible. That's right, darling,
that's the mystery of the mouth."

Leopard dog wags his tail.
THIS IS GOOD, he says.

"Shut up. You're a stupid dog," I say. "What do you know?"

I KNOW YES AND NO
AND *BOW WOW.* GOOD DOG,
BAD DOG. I KNOW PLAY
AND STAY. LICK I KNOW
AND SNIFF I KNOW. *BOW WOW,*
BOW WOW, WHAT DO YOU KNOW?

"Who's that?" Father yells.

> *That's just Leopard. He knows we're in here,*
> *He's lonely. Darling, would you mind?*
> *He likes to watch.*

"What?"

> *You know what I'm saying. He's just a dog.*

3. *The Holiness in Sex*

GR-R-R— Leopard on his haunches
peeping through the keyhole.

"Hey, move over, Dog, scram!"

Leopard Dog snaps at my hand,
   eyes like cracked glass.

LOOK OUT. I EAT LITTLE BOYS FOR BREAKFAST!

"The socks come off and the feet talk," Father says.

YOUR FATHER'S ALL MUSCLE.
WHO WOULD HAVE THOUGHT?
LENORE LIKES THAT. THEY'RE A MATCH.
THAT'S YOUR NEW MOTHER.

"The way to heaven is not up, but down.
Love—marriage—intercourse, what are they, darling?
A tangling of toes, right?
                        So, how does this feel, Lenore?
Good... and this?"

                    Oh, doctor, doctor... You know,
                    I like professional men... full of surprises.
                    Crazy talk. Silly exams... touching...
                    and nice pajamas.

THERE THEY GO, SONNY.

"The holiness derives from feeling the pleasure," Father says.
"No pleasure, no holiness."

OOO, WICKY, WICKY, says Leopard Dog,
THAT'S HOW YOU WERE MADE, LITTLE BOY.
NO WICKY WICKY, NO LITTLE BOY.

"Move, darling, move, you need to move!"

LOOK AT THAT. IT'S HEELS OVER BEDPOSTS.
IT'S WICKY WICKY HE LOVES, NOT YOU, SONNY.

4. Lenore Gets on Top

Father sits on the side of the bed
        whinnying like a horse,
stepmother neighing softly.

"So look at us," he says,
        reaching for her.
"we're invisible, that's what we are."

                Invisible?

"Invisible, yes: no boundary between exterior and interior.
Tell me, darling, where do I leave off and you begin?

Inside you is inside me. Outside you is outside me.
We're both the same.
So, *nu,* who sees that? Who sees us? We're invisible."

> *Luftmensch, head in the clouds.*
> *You miss this, doctor, and you miss that.*
> *You think that make you a mystic?*
> *Invisible? I'll show you invisible.*

WHAT, YOU STILL DON'T GET IT? says Dog,
> thwacking me with his tail.
LENORE'S YOUR MOMMY, LITTLE BOY,
WICKY WICKY'S YOUR FATHER.
YOU HAD A MOTHER.
NOW YOU HAVE ANOTHER.

Hands on his shoulders, she sits on father,
moves up and down.

> *Now you see it, now you don't, she says.*

BAD LENORE, BAD. THAT'S NOT DOG, says Dog,
> barking at the keyhole.

"There is man and woman and a third thing, too,
in us, says the poet*. That's the eye in the heart
that sees into the invisible. The goal, Poet says, is to see
with the eye of the heart so like sees like."

> *Shut up, she says, shut up and schtepp.*

"Oh God, marry me," he says, "marry me."

---

*Jelaluddin Rumi.

GOD IS A PEDESTRIAN

Palm Springs, CA

Podiatrist:

"Trust water, son, you can't go wrong with water.
See, and it's got dual arm rests,
multi-directional
        massage jets,
pneumatic air switch,
a four-horsepower motor

"So, hold here, hold the grab bar—
get in, son. Take a ride on the plumbing express!

"Good for the feet,
good for the back.
Foot problems,
back problems,
        they go together!"

I'm swept away.

"Schlimazel! Hydrotherapy is your friend. Hold the grab bar.
        You want to know a secret?"

            Please, dad, no philosophy.

"God is a pedestrian. God who is in heaven
        is also a man, just like you and me."

            And what about angels?

"I'm telling you, if they looked after their feet
        they wouldn't need to fly."

            Dad, you're nuts.

"Of course, everything is imagination. Rosicrucian says."

            Rosicrucian?

"One saw the world in a grain of sand.
So, *nu?* I see it in a pair of feet."

No, dad, not feet again.

"Yes, feet. Feet. The sun and the moon and the stars.
Feet, feet are heaven, too, a heaven filled with stars.
Rosicrucian says. The world is a man and the light of the sun
and the stars is his body."

This is Rosicrucian?

"Goyisheh kop! Think! The two are one:
God exists in man so body is a form of soul.
Heal the soul and you heal the body.
Heal the foot and you heal the soul.
That world is in this world, and this world is in that."

So what are you saying, dad?
Maybe there is no 'other side.'

"What am I saying? Wake up!
This is the other side. You're there," he says,
handing me a towel, "right
here, right now. You're home."

HE TAKES ME BACK AS A PATIENT

"So there they are, on a pedestal
            your feet under lights.
More than you deserve,
you and those prima donnas.
Villains!" He points a finger.
"With normal people the socks come off
            and the feet talk. But not these two.
Wise guys. Too good for diagnosis, huh?
Too good for arch supports? Is that it?

"Your X-ray shows nothing. Ultra-sound
            nothing.
This is your last chance. This is it.

Weak ankles, feet out of alignment,
        but there's something else.
I see it in your posture. You're holding back,
        you and those feet of yours,
                slippery feet,
meshugge feet,
        feet like no one else in the family.
What's going on in there?" he asks.
"Wake up! Tell you what:
we're gonna have you walk around the office.
That's it. Head erect,
        back straight.
No, no! Look at you, look at you: you call that walking?
On the ground, on the ground!
Dreamer! *Ach!* You're fired! Your mother was right.
You and those feet of yours are two of a kind."

HEAVENLY SEX

1. The Law

Opens a bottle of schnapps. "Writer, *schmyter,*
you're unemployed.
Unemployed people must make love
at least once a day.
Talmud says:
        A laborer, twice a week; a mule driver
once a week; a camel driver,
once a month. It's the law.
        This is heavenly sex. Say a blessing—
pray— 'Blessed art thou, O Lord our God...'
Ba-ruch a-ta Adonai, El-lo-hei-nu...
For your spouse and for your seed.
What is it with you?
I need to explain how to bring a soul into the world?"

2. The Blessing

"Listen:
The soul is the Lord's candle.
So you say a blessing. And you sing to her—your wife:

Strength and honor are her clothing, you sing.
She openeth her mouth with wisdom, you sing.
Her children arise up and call her blessed, you sing.
Rabbi says if knowing a woman were not holy,
        it would not be called 'knowing.'
So, after a good *Shabbes* meal—
        linen tablecloth, blessed spices,
braided loaves of *challah,*
        a goblet of wine...
Thirty-nine things you cannot do on the Sabbath,
but you can eat. You can drink. You can *schtepp.*
Make one another happy.
It's the law."

WEDDING #2

       i.

Temple Parking Lot

My father says:
"So, my son is getting married!"

      For the second time, dad.

"Yes, but weddings heal. Our Talmud says
a wedding frees bride and groom
      from all past transgressions.
A wedding fixes all that's broken."

      You mean one marriage can fix another?

He grabs my arm: "A happy marriage
gives eternal dispensation."

His eyes gather light.
"The Talmud says intercourse is one-sixtieth
the pleasure of paradise."

I'm wearing five-eyelet Florsheims
      with new arch supports.

"This is good." He waves to friends.
"Just don't fumble the goblet."

The goblet?

"The goblet you break after the vows.
This time use your heel. Smash it on the first try.
People'll be watching. Miss it and they'll laugh—
          like last time.
Don't fumble the goblet."

ii.
Temple Steps

Leads with his chin.
Visible and invisible.
Chin trembling, his face shining.

"I was an orphan."

Yes, I know, dad.

"Did you know an orphan's dead parents
are able to attend the wedding?"

But dad, I'm not an orphan.

"Well, I just want you to know if you were,
          we'd come anyway.
You know, your grandparents will be there too."

How will they manage that?

"What are you asking? They'll manage.
These are your grandparents:
Grandpa Hyman. Grandmother Bessie.
It's a tradition. Our Talmud says
if they have their bodies, they'll come with their bodies."

But they're dead.

"So, they'll come without."

iii.
Temple Washroom

"When a man unites with his wife,
God is between them.
I'm telling you: lovemaking is ceremony.
The Talmud says.
You, you're not holy, but your wife is.
With her
        you go to a world outside the world."

                So?

"So wash your hands before
        not after.
Wash for the pure and holy bride."

                But what about hygiene?

"How did I bring you up?
Shame on you.
The socks come off and you make love.
The Talmud says. And you make her happy.
Schtepp. Schtepp. Do you understand?
Forget hygiene!
This is the pure and holy bride."

MARRIAGE #3

"Again? That's it.
This time marriage divorces you.
Just walk, walk now, keep walking.
Dr. Neusome's son eats and becomes sensible.
Horse radish, bagels, lox, cream cheese—
A *mensch*. Honorable.
But you, horseradish turns into what?
Divorce.
Bagels into divorce. Cream cheese
into divorce.
You know *schlemiel?* A *schlemiel* trips
        and knocks down the *schlimazel*.

So which are you?
A love weasel, that's what you are.
He obtains a blessing, beautiful
        young woman,
and out it comes, divorce.
With each divorce the *mensch* in you
        gets split in two.
And there's no money in it.
Divide down the middle,
        right down the middle,
Half of a half of a half...
The middle? This time
        there is no middle.
And now the yoga...
The podiatrist's son walks now on his head.
Another blessing. Head over heels didn't work. So, *nu,*
now it's heels over head.
Yes, feet in the clouds, *ach.*
Such a blessing!
Fine, fine! Stand on your head if you like.
Some part of you at least will touch the ground."

MARRIAGE #4

Palm Springs, CA

"One, two, three... Shame
And more children than you can count.
Meshugge.
What have you learned? And now a fourth.
Everything in the world has meaning.
        So, *nu,* tell me:
What's the meaning of this?
Earth, air, fire and foolishness...
The sun and the moon and the stars.
These I understand.
Hieroglyphics I understand.
But you! How many times does a foot marry a foot?
A man should tangle feet with one woman.
One pair of feet. One family. One home.
How many do you need?

'How's your son?' Mrs. Goldberg asks me.
'Fine, fine,' I say. 'He's getting married.'
'Ah, mazel tov, doctor!'
Three years later she says,
'So, how's the boy?'
'Fine, fine. He's married again.'
'Oi vay!' she says, 'children…'
         She's been through it too.
People say it's human to want to put an end to things.
Well, not for those with their feet on the ground.
Look at your clever face in the mirror: Look,
         look at yourself. Now count:
one face, one face you see, not four.
So, better that part of you with brains
should take off its socks and study feet. For that…
you don't need a mirror."

AFTER THE BYPASS

Palm Springs, CA

1. In The Hospital

"Don't trust the world, son. It's filled
with holes. The best thing is to love…"

Love what, dad?

"Emptiness. I've been meaning to tell you:
There's a giant scroll suspended below the world
         and it says this world
         is made from letters and numbers
and every number is infinite.
Anyway, I'm invisible, son."

Dad, I can see you.

"You have two fathers,
         one you can see,
one who looks like me;
         and one you can't,

the father you'll never see.
The invisible is invisible,
but I need to make a living.
I'm a doctor, *nu?* What good is a doctor
if you can't see him?
Don't look at me like that. I'm still a Jew,
but some days all I see is Roses and Crosses.
Did you know the human body has nine holes in it?
Seven of those holes are in the head. So there you have it.
The world is a leaky boat, son."

2. Checking Out

Rosy cheek father in a wheel chair.
He pulls out a toothpick. Makes little sucking noises
with his teeth. "Hospital food. Not as bad as they say."

Lights a cigarette.

"She's against it."
                        Who?

"Who do you think? She's against
the invisible."

Throws away the toothpick.

"I've fallen into a place where everything is music.
You know, if people could take a pill
and become invisible
there would be nobody in sight. It's true. The world
        is made of love,
of our love for emptiness.
Ach, what the hell! Visible, invisible,
        It's all the same.
Still, the world you go round thinking you can see
is filled with holes, and for every hole
        in this world
        there's a hole in the other. If you look,
you can see through the cracks.
I have a treasure now, it's true,
        but no body.

And you, you *meshugge,* you have a body,
but no treasure.
You should take the year off. Spend some time
at the Invisible College."

3. Course of Study

Lesson #1

"Stars ejaculate. That's how the world
            came into being.
From sperm. The Sperm of the Stars."

Lesson #2

"There is no place empty of God.

"Darkness is a candle, too.

"So open the window in your chest.
Let the invisible fly in and out."

Lesson #3

"The invisible is more existent than all the visible things.
Talmud says.
Still, when you leave your body there's not much to stand on.
And there's a crack in the cosmic egg.
Truth is, this world is just one side of the nothing
That's on the other side."

Lesson #4

"Now I'll tell you about death.
Life has an eye to see, says Talmud,
                but what do you think Death has?
Death is made of eyes,
                made of eyes, dressed in eyes.
And when she comes, she comes with a knife
        in her hands.
And you go through the wall and it's a flaming word.

Death is what happens when all you have left
      is the life that was there all along.
But remember: you're still gonna need money
      when you die."

A MAN NEEDS A PLACE TO STAND

Father:

"Snap out of it, son!
      Yes, of course I'm dead,
but you think I've left the world?
Then how come you're talking to me?
Nu? ask yourself:
      How is this possible? Listen to me:
There's more good news.
That's right: Death doesn't separate you from God.
      This is a surprise? You were thinking
          there's something to fear?
Anyway, wait'll you die, son. You'll see.
We never entirely leave the world.
Ach, there's no 'there' to leave. There's hardly a 'here.'
And you, *nudnik,*
      you just think you have a body.
Still, you can't chase the invisible.
Do that and you'll end up everywhere,
      and then what?
A man needs a place to stand."

LIFE IS ITS OWN AFTERLIFE

"Enough already. Mourn,
      mourn all you want...
What good will it do?
Truth is, I feel great, son. Never better!

"So what if I'm invisible?
So what if I'm dead?
You don't need a body to be a *mensch,*
      a man of substance.

Ach, but with a body at least
you've got some privacy.
Without a body you can't conceal anything.

"There's more, son,
   and bad news for you.
God, —this will surprise you—
when you die one of the first questions He asks is,
   'Did you marry?'
Turns out after God created the world, the rest of the time
He spent making marriages.
So a couple, when they meet, it's *bashert,*
   'it was meant to be.'
That's so... that's how
   together they fulfill their destiny.
But divorce, that they don't allow.
So you won't be coming.

     But thank God
   for what you've got.
What are you missing? Not much. There is no afterlife,
   not really.
That's right, son.
Life is its own afterlife."

HIS FATHER SAYS

1.

"What? I'll give you depression.
I'll give you to die. Goddammit,
it's not enough I'm dead?
I got to worry about you too?
True, you're not your body.
But you're not your mind either.
So die, I say. That's right. Strip the soul away
   and you'll see
there is no death. Death,
death is when the soul
and the feet part company.
That's all.

But you can pray. Only remember, son:
Prayer is wordless.
If it's got words, it's not prayer."

2.

"Thoughts have souls.
Souls have souls.
Everything's a covering.
What are you covering
With that mug of yours?
All those wives, and worse
those children you left,
gonif you are, a thief
Who steals happiness.
You think you're broken.
You think the world is broken.
Ach, enough. Snap out of it. Just snap *out* of it!"

3.

"You want the name of God
to be rubbed away from your forehead?
Wake up, wake up!
                    Tell me,
What is a human being?
What makes a person a person?"

"I see the other side of nothing is nothing, Dad."

"Ach, you and that brain of yours,
30 billion neurons it contains,
a million billion connections,
and look at you, look at you—
                    mishegoss, looney bin—
          a face to sadden God.

"Think about it. You're only visiting your life, you know.
Why not live like you were still among the living?
Die if you're going to die, young man,
but don't start eternity being depressed."

SPANISH BAY, PEBBLE BEACH, CARMEL-BY-THE SEA

Jacuzzis jet fresh-minted Yummy
in your suite at the Nouveau Riche Hotel.
Spanish Bay, Pebble Beach, Carmel-by-the Sea.

A waiter brings hummingbird tongues, Tiffany
single malt whiskey, leather-buttocked Gucci belle—
edible, delectable—from the Mall in the Sky.

Male female limousines tummy to tummy
champagne blue chip grilled gazelle for Senator Swell.
Nothing tastes better than new-minted money.

Bing Crosby caviar, a summer's bounty.
A chorus of Junior Leaguers swathed in labels.
Welcome to the Golden Calf. Bow to Givenchy,
AT&T, Celebrity Worship By-The-Sea.

WEDDING SONG

>   —For Kamala

1. Maika'i Kaua'i, Beautiful Kaua'i

White blue crayola-green island,
      Emerald Garden,
          circular
    black lava, turtle shell Eden,
Eden with a thousand waterfalls,
sixty million year old 'shield volcano,'
      its weight sealing the fissure below.

Elvis was here for the filming of *Blue Hawaii,*

>   *(Hug me a heap,*
>   *love me a lot,*
>   *rock the hula, baby,*
>   *rock rock rock)*

At its center, Mt. Waialeale, 5,100 feet,
       rain magnet,
wettest spot on earth.

      Lovers in the movie "Thorn Birds",
      lovers in "South Pacific,"
         and "King Kong" too
      tearing up the landscape
      looking for love.

2. The Groom

        conjuror,
        hazel-eyed magus
        body of a dancer

"...birthplace of the hula
      and home to Laka,
         goddess of the dance."

        cloudburst, flower, tree
        dream wish, dream forest—
        remembered paradise—

"A saying and a binding,

      birth of marriage
        and prayer
           for the green earth."

3. The Bride Gives Directions

"Nothing marks the route," she says,
my slender,
      mercurial, dark hair,
           dove-eyed daughter
        facing east,
    sunlit
     facing in all directions,
all at once giving back light
in all directions.

Herself an Eden,
  she is a garden
    enclosed in a garden,
a fountain of gardens.

Calls us to Eden.

     * * *

Wedding with fruit and stringed instruments,
wedding as awakening,

bisque white sea foam

white night-blooming jasmine,
water lilies
  shaken by a breeze named
'scent-bearer,'
   then a second breeze
    and a third.

4. A Father's Offering

   head lei of close-pressed flowers,
   a piece of star fruit,
   a mango wrapped
    in ti leaf.

Kamala, Lotus
sunlit daughter on a sun-struck island.

    —Hanalei, Kaua'i, Hawaii - September 9, 1999

With thanks to James Houston.

ONE FOR THE ROAD

One for the road.
A little detached it was, but bouncy, flouncy, hoochie coochie,
woo wah woo, out there under the stars,
woo wah woo,
one for the road, one for the road it was,
and end of the show.
Stupid shit, how was I to know?
One for the road and end of the show?
So good-humored it was, I missed the clue,
hugging and kissing, all that
hugging and kissing.
Missed just how all over it really was.

TURNING 60

> *The first 40 years of life give us the text;*
> *the next 30 supply the commentary on it...*
> —Schopenhauer

1. Homework

According to Webster, the word six derives from the Latin
"sex" [s-e-x] and the Greek "hex" [h-e-x].
Six units or members
as, an ice-hockey team;
a 6-cylinder engine;
six fold, six-pack, sixpenny nail, six-
shooter, sixth sense.

"Zero" denotes the absence of all magnitude, the point of departure
in reckoning; the point from which the graduation of a scale
(as of a thermometer) begins;
zero hour,
zeroth,
as, "the zero power of a number."

Zero, the great "there's nothing there" number,
a blast off into a new decade.

2. Grammar as Hymnal

Seeking solace in a review of grammar, I turned to Strunk & White's
Elements of Style. Standing at attention,
opening to the section on usage, I chanted and sang –
uniting my voice with the voices of others, the vast chorus
of the lovers of English.

We sing of verb tense, past, present and future.
We sing the harmony of simple tenses.
We lift our voice in praise of action words,
        and the function of verb tense.

We sing of grammar which is our compass
providing, as it does, clues as to how
we might navigate the future,
at the same time it
illuminates the past.

As a teacher, I talk. That's present.
For thirty years as a teacher, I talked. That's past.
It may only be part time, but I will talk. That's future.

3. Living the Future Perfect

I will have invoked the muse.

I will have remembered to give thanks, knowing our origins
are in the invisible, and that we once possessed boundless energy,
but were formless, and that we are here to know 'the things of the heart
through touching.'

I will have remembered, too, that there is only one thing
we all possess equally and that is our loneliness.

I will have loved.
You will have loved.
We will have loved.

APPENDIX

INTRODUCTION TO *KISSING THE DANCER*, 1964
BY (PULITZER PRIZE WINNER) WILLIAM MEREDITH

These poems are unusual and excellent in a number of ways, but what strikes me first about them is that they are the only book of poems I know about—well, maybe one of two I know about—that has been turned down by a lot of publishers over a good many years because they are so original as to be unrecognizable as poetry by a conventional eye. They have gone off to respectable publishers with praise from Stanley Kunitz, Louise Bogan, even Robert Lowell, and come back with the embarrassed confession that they simply escaped the respectable editors. I submit that this is very rare today, when so many books of poems are printed every month and the squarest publishers are looking for poetry with the dogged altruism of philanthropists.

Randall Jarrell recently described a school of prosperous, mild-talented poets as seeming to have come out of the lining of Richard Wilbur's overcoat. The poets of another school, who appear to get into print pretty easily, strike me as having their home at the bottom of William Carlos Williams' laundry hamper. You cannot recognize Robert Sward's poems by any such affinity. They come out of original experience and they exist in language that the experience discovered. And if that is the least that can be said of any book of real poems, it means more when a book presents experience as odd as this one does. I was tempted to the impertinence of this introduction because I was curious to see if I could say why these poems have delighted and puzzled me for six years.

From reading Robert Frost I have learned to look for giveaway lines in poems, hidden lines that tell the sly reader some of the secrets by which a poet works. "The bird would cease and be as other birds / But that he knows in singing not to sing," in "The Oven Bird" are two such lines. With Sward these secret lines are not only hidden but often apparently in the negative, recounting apparent creative errors. "My examples are all myself," he says, implying that that's wrong. But the poem "For Charlie," where the line occurs, shows that in fact it's right: that once you get a good fierce look at the example of self—the only example any of us will ever have—you can see the world in it. I think Sward believes that.

And he writes (in "All For A Day"):

"All day I have written words;
My subject has been that. Words.
And I am wrong. And the words."

But there are a hundred lines in this book which seem to have found their sweet, eccentric selves in this very preoccupation. Certain entire poems like "In Cities" (and perhaps "All For A Day" itself) take life from a fierce intensity of verbal attention.

And here is a stanza that can probably be taken at its face value as poetics, although I'm not saying it will make the problem of writing poems a whole lot easier for any of us:

> "I am fond of death—and/or
> The self-contained. This poem may not be said to be
> About souls. But of things. Feathers and leaves.
> Leafless trees and the featherless bodies of crows.
> Finally, let us say, I have been asked to write
> simply."

As nearly as we can ever know these things about one another, I know that Robert Sward works long and hard on his poems. I have asked myself, What does he work on about them? I mean, they don't rhyme or scan, like some of my glossy works, and they don't allude to American History. I have come to the conclusion that when he works on them he is paying perfect, slightly mystical attention to the things he's tipped us off to above: (1) himself as an example of a man; (2) his vocabulary as a butterfly net to catch the experiences the man has; and (3) a passion for simplicity. His simplicity is not that of Zen (now there's a gamy laundry hamper to breed poets in) or of Thoreau, but something more like that of Blake or Emily Dickinson. If you look at things long enough with this kind of attention they sometimes resolve themselves into pure creation: you find yourself using italics, 'and they're not yours—they're created italics.' Here is a section of a poem called "Scenes From A Text," which has the fairly hair-raising epigraph "'Several actual, potentially and/or really traumatic situations are depicted on these pages.' —Transient Personality Reactions to Acute or Special Stress (Chapter 5)."

> "Photo II
>
> "The house is burning. The furniture
> Is scattered on the lawn (tables, chairs
> TV, refrigerator). Momma—
> There is a small, superimposed white
> Arrow pointed at her—is busy
> Tearing out her eyes. The mute husband
> (Named, arrowed) stands idly by, his hands
> Upon his hips, eyes already out.

'The smoke blankets the sky.' And the scene,
Apart from Momma, Poppa, the flames…
Could be an auction. Friends, relatives
Neighbors, all stand by, reaching, fighting
For the mirrors, TV, sunglasses;
The children, the cats and speechless dogs."

Like other good works of art, these poems have the air of having been made for people rather than for other artists. They contain high-toned gossip rather than aesthetics, or the aesthetics are hidden and acted out like charades. A lot of the poems are unpleasant in places, like life itself, but none of them contains any fashionable despair. No claim is advanced that our time is more terrible or hopeless than another or, on the other hand, that you and I don't have experience as the poet has experience. There is that humility about them that comes from paying a blasphemous attention, God's own attention, to oneself. I myself couldn't work that way, and I couldn't have written this book, but I think I will soon be in good company when I say I much admire it.

—WILLIAM MEREDITH, 1964

FOREWORD TO *HORGBORTOM STRINGBOTTOM / I AM YOURS / YOU ARE HISTORY,* 1970

"In progress since 1965, sections of this book-length poem have appeared in periodicals under two working titles: *In Mexico* (which applies to the place of the poem's origin and the landscape in which a number of the lyrics and refrain are rooted—along with the American Southwest) and *Which Way, Which Way to the Revolution?* (which derives from the section titled *Dreams* and that sets the tone for parts III and IV). The poem was first conceived as a 100-page broadsheet and collage for a chorus of 50 or more voices—among them Orphan Annie, Dick Tracy, Mamie Eisenhower, Minotaur, waterskiers, etc.—all of them, innocent and horrendous, in a groping and violent evolutionary state. Begun in Mexico, *Horgbortom* was completed in Spring, 1969, in New Hampshire with the prospect of the work appearing with the author again outside the States…"

"Concert" and "In Mexico" first appeared in *Poetry Chicago, 1966.* "In Mexico" reprinted in *Where Is Vietnam: American Poets Respond,* ed. Walter Lowenfels. Both were later revised for inclusion in *Horgbortom Stringbottom,* 1970.

Back cover copy by the publisher (Swallow Press) described *Horgbortom* as a "long, choric poem… a recording from other countries and from the context of America itself of fantasy, song, and apocalypse, five years [1965-1970], not so much of revolution as the first rumblings..."

Swallow Press also noted "This book is political in a way that only poetry can be, addressing itself with full attention to images of ourselves that our culture and state press into our waking and our dreams and moving, as it catches its own special language, away from them and toward a surviving personal declaration."

INTRODUCTION TO *POET SANTA CRUZ*, 1985
BY MORTON MARCUS

It is always of more than passing interest when a poet of note changes direction, as Robert Sward is doing now. Sward has been a unique figure on the North American poetry scene for almost twenty years, publishing a number of highly original books and chapbooks in the U.S., Canada, and Europe.

Up to now, he has been known for his anarchic exuberance and existential outlook, confronting a universe of chaotic nothingness with a whoop and a holler and an embattled good humor best exemplified in such well-known pieces as "Hello Poem" and his remembrance of childhood, "Uncle Dog: The Poet At 9."

Sward has placed his chips on Love, Language, and the Imagination and let the cosmic roulette wheel spin. He grabbed Nothingness by the ears and kissed it with a loud smack flush on the face, and even tried to seduce Death in such poems as "Statement of Poetics or 'Goodbye To Myself.'"

Now he has moved from Canada to California, taken up residence at Santa Cruz County's Mt. Madonna Center, and the physical and psychical environment has taken him by the tongue to new spiritual heights, which have slowed his responses to a meditative stillness and (surprisingly) eased him back into such closed forms as sonnets and villanelles, while giving him an interest in subjects East Indian and Chinese.

A long-time practitioner of yoga, who found in the process a sense of communion with the self and others, Sward has discovered at Mt. Madonna an increased depth of vision. This change shows in his new poems, "A Monk On The Santa Cruz Mountain"; "Castroville, California—A Coffee Shop..."; and "Li Po."

The exuberance and humor are still there, but they are now augmented by a more sober tone of resignation that can only be born of a different kind of understanding, one that seems to be moving the poet toward a hard won serenity.

—MORTON MARCUS, 1985

INTRODUCTION TO *ROSICRUCIAN IN THE BASEMENT*, 2001, BY WILLIAM MINOR

The appearance of a new book of poems by Robert Sward is a significant event—one uncompromised by the place this book will eventually take in the already impressive body of work he has afforded his readers.

Rosicrucian in the Basement is of special significance for a poet whose mature work has been hailed by Carolyn Kizer as "fresh, ingenuous, and funnier than ever." The poet, with customary generosity, is offering a book so filled with love (enhanced by artistic skill) that this simple four-letter word is rendered fully plausible, accessible, redeemed. The problems that lesser practitioners too often fall into while addressing the topic—insincerity or self-aggrandizement—are simply not present here, and what we are left with is The Real Thing, in all its humble glory—not as an object apart, but the life of our life.

Robert Sward is also a master at: (1) astonishing long term fans, such as myself, with his ongoing capacity for variety and surprise; (2) presenting abstruse or complex concerns in a manner that is refreshingly straightforward, even simple, and (3) telling a story, providing a continuous narrative thread, yet remaining totally lyrical at the same time.

On the first count, Watch out! Although Robert is a proven, prolific, veteran performer, he has a way—like first-rate jazz improvisers—of keeping everybody on their toes. You're never quite sure just where he's going to go next, but when he gets there, the move—no matter how audacious at the time— was the right move: the result of seasoned versatility combined with a willingness to seek out new directions at considerable risk.

Not too long ago, I heard guitarist Bill Frisell at the Monterey Jazz Festival. I was surprised to find myself comparing the poems that make up Robert's book, which I had just read, with the work of this constantly evolving, incessantly surprising and delighting musician. Jazz critics have commented on Frisell's "unusual tonal colors," his playfulness and humor ("an eerie sense of funhouse mirrors"), his talent for surprise ("a Pandora's box of unexpected sounds and twisting mercurial lines"), and his ability to combine a laid-back, down home ("the happier strains of an American yesterday") approach with a totally contemporaneous sound ("tastefully minimal flashes of electronic sleight of hand"). I was tempted to borrow or steal such phrases of praise and apply them to Robert Sward's latest poems (and I just did!), for Robert, like Bill Frisell, has the unique ability to take us to some Great Good Place of his own devising, but one with a slight and occasionally fearful edge to it—keeping his readers (or listeners) constantly alert and alive.

Hearing Bill Frisell, I had a vision of my Arkansas father, no longer alive, speaking to me from whatever quarters he now inhabits, saying (and with the thick accent he never lost on earth and I'm sure he still retains), "Bill, I am pleased to see that at long last you have finally found some of that there jazz music that even I can appreciate!" And I can hear my father, having read Robert Sward's latest poems, saying the same thing about what he used to call "poultry." While on the surface they may not appear to have much in common, I think my father and the "father" of Robert's poems would get along quite well—just as the country-minimalism, or what one critic has called "porch music," of Bill Frisell is fully compatible with the podiatry-based wisdom of Robert's *Rosicrucian in the Basement*.

The ability to present highly complex concerns and insights in a straightforward, accessible manner—to create poems that grow increasingly "baroque" in their very economy (a trait the Japanese call *yugen,* a preference for suggestion over overt statement)—is a gift that Robert Sward is willing to share with us in his new work—alongwith the third ingredient I mentioned: a nearly miraculous ability to blend straight narration and lyricism: to create a genre all his own that combines and transcends any cramped distinctions between prose and poetry. It's not an easy feat, technically or otherwise. When I try this in my own work, I tend to slip into what people regard as strictly prose (the "poetry," they say, drops out). Yet Robert somehow manages to juggle both worlds until they blur, blessedly, into a single form of continuous delight. The "characters" presented become indelible, as in fine fiction; the settings vivid in their detail, yet the "music" never stops—the poems filled as they are with infectious rhythms, touchstone phrases, and delectable juxtapositions.

So welcome to the amazing universe of Robert Sward, with all of its fresh and surprising twists and turns this time out: a world that probes more deeply (than perhaps it has dared to before) into the troublesome (and endlessly rewarding) terrain of metaphysics—eternity placed just where it should be, embedded in the here and now; the slightly demonic firmly rooted in the divine. Welcome to a set of philosophical and religious concerns that never lose sight of the all-too-human (and endlessly rewarding also) desire to delight and entertain. Above all, welcome to a world rife with love as it really is: teasing, tantalizing, torturous at times, yet full of infinite possibility and—if I may be permitted this phrase a third time—endlessly rewarding.

Be prepared to meet the whole "family," and to accept an invitation to step into their shoes. I guarantee you'll never forget the experience. "Too good for feet? Here, son, try walking in these."

—WILLIAM MINOR, 2001

EPILOGUE

Robert Sward is the master of the logical incongruity—the very essence of surprise and delight in poetry. He is a compassionate storyteller who looks at life through the sincerity and profundity of genuine wit, always rising above the ordinary, the mundane and the despairing. Beneath every poem lies a playful metaphysics, a melodious ear, and the exacting ability to tear down that artificial barrier that exists between the reader and the poems. It is a joy to walk in the world of Sward's perceptions and to discover the wonder that inspires each poem.

Take for example a poem such as "A Walk in the A Scenery." One moment Sward is pointing out to us something he has noticed, and the next we are part of the very scene he has directed our eye toward. I am reminded of the playfulness, not only of Apollinaire, but of that marvelous scene in *Mary Poppins* where the Banks children leap into a sidewalk chalk drawing. In poetry there should not be that barrier of artificiality which all too often interjects itself between the reader and the work. What Sward manages time and time again in his poetry is to break down that barrier. He makes his poems engaging to the point where we are not only invited to partake of them, but in them. And herein lies the secret behind Robert Sward's incredible opus: he is not just a poet but a poet who guides his reader. What William Meredith may have mistaken for the "unusual" when he wrote his introduction to Sward's first book of poems, *Kissing the Dancer* (1964), is not unusual at all: it is just unexpected, and Sward always relishes the opportunity to point out such things. As a poet, at first glance he appears to be almost a jack-in-a-box who has learned how to crank his own handle; yet every time he leaps out we remain surprised and pleased, and the pop is always accompanied by "Look here!" And we do.

Whenever the word guide comes up one automatically thinks of Virgil leading Dante through Hell. On our right we have the Fraud artists, and on our left the Sodomites... In essence, what Dante is allowing his recreated Roman poet to do is to train the eye by acting as pointer to unexpected recognitions and understandings that we might not notice on our own. That's Dante being didactic. Sward is different. He loves to point things out to us, but they are things that he himself has just suddenly become aware of. There is a strong presence of epiphany throughout his works. His is the voice of the dreamer who has awakened to the moment of astonishment. What is incredible is that he has spent a lifetime in astonishment. There have been so many times when I have spoken to Robert over lunches or during long phone conversations between Toronto and

California when he has uttered the phrase "Wow!" Each new recognition seems to bring a wave of exuberance to him.

Robert Sward has led a life of discovery. He was born in Chicago in 1933, the son of a Jewish doctor. He has always struck me as someone who has inherited an analytical, if not diagnostic mind—the sort of brain that tries to figure out what it is seeing and explain it. As one reads through these poems there is a sense, however, that science would have been too limiting for Sward. The playful expanse of metaphor seems more to his ilk. At the age of seventeen, he joined the United States Navy and served in Korea aboard a "three hundred foot LST (landing ship tank), and was placed in charge of a small, but rather well-constructed library of twelve hundred books. It was while at sea that he began writing poems. Sward seems to have loved the navy because a) it presented him with a moveable library that he seems to have consumed ravenously; and b) it offered him the chance to indulge his spirit of discovery.

This spirit of discovery, which could very easily be assigned to the fact that Sward is a career academic who has taught at Cornell, Iowa, the University of Victoria, and UC Santa Cruz, goes deeper than mere book learning. There's an ocean inside Sward and he is constantly attempting to plumb its depths in search of intellectual, physical and spiritual meaning. In some of his most moving poems such as "Chicago's Walheim Cemetery," he struggles to find the depth within himself that will enable him to shed tears: "Now, I too will attempt tears. / They are like song. They are like flight. / I fail." Yet the mere recognition of the failure is contact with the poet's duende. In other poems, where he comes face to face with the unfamiliar, such as "Impossible Hurricane Loss-of-Name Poem," Sward asks "If I dig a hole will I find a poem? / A pot of unicorns? / A herd of leprechauns? / I ask. The rainbow has already moved." Sward never met a trope he didn't like. In the hands of a lesser artist, such a gift would be a disaster. The poem, however, concludes, "O name poor name, / will the rain care for you as I have cared for you? / Will the wind devour you, / knock your head against a tree? / Already I have forgotten." Such poems are more than mere tropery. They go beyond the conceit. They enter the realm of the mystical where reality and understanding fuse in that rare and often inexplicable sense of wonder and understanding that offers us meaning and sustenance.

Sward lists among his hobbies "swimming, meditating, yoga and computers," three of the most spiritual and metaphysical activities I can think of. The critic Lawrence Lieberman once pointed out that in Sward's poetry "the mysticism of objects, of thingness is and inversion and create a bizarre parody of conventional mysticism. With Wordsworth, we 'see into the life of things.' In Sward's world, things work their way inside our life, become parts of our psyche, dominate our minds and take us over, make us over, entirely." For Sward, the ability to see into things is a two-way street, and just as we can pop into the landscape, the landscape can, just as easily, pop into us. I wouldn't venture to call him a romantic. That would be too mundane. What I would cite, however, is the passionate and innate mysticism that Sward seems to have developed through in his poetry.

Whenever I pick up works by Rumi, I am always reminded of Sward's poetry—not just because he was the one who turned me on to that ancient Afghani but because, like Rumi, Sward is a poet of enlightened conversation. Rumi spent his life seeking the other, the one with whom he could have an enduring conversation, the dialogue of self and soul through which one makes the discovery of something far more beautiful than the merely observable. Take a look at Sward's poems: many are, at first glance, quoted monologues, the voices of those he has heard and absorbed during his life time. They are all in search of an understanding of their place in the universe, both the subjective inner universe and the objective outer universe. But look closer. These are not just monologues. These are dialogues, and in such dialogues the conversations are not just addressed to the persona of the poems but to the reader. Yes, Sward is a poetic eavesdropper, but in his engaging opus, so are we. And by listening to what each voice has to say, we see not only into the souls of others but into our own inner lives.

When I used the term "logical incongruity" I meant it in the highest possible sense of praise for a poet. Logic helps us to see our way into the poet's reality, but it is the very sense of the incongruous, the unexpected surprise, the inversion of relationship between images and objects, the metaphor that dares to flirt with fallacy but which conquers fallacy through the power of brilliant associate: these are the attributes of logical incongruity. In those poems where Sward looks at the world through the eyes of a dog, there is much more at work than humor or even the wide-eyed, tail-wagging innocence that a poet must have if he or she is to endure the cruelties of the world that must be observed. What is at work is a spiritual courage that declares to all who will listen, "the impossible is possible because I believe it can be." Such a stance might seem incongruous, but it is the poet's craft, his ear, his joy of language, and his ability to give voice to the other, that brings to this symphony of utterance the blessed order we all rage for. Incongruous, yes. Logical, yes. And throughout it all, there is Sward acting as our guide, one ear bent to listen as the words spring to life, and the other ear waiting patiently for our response.

—PROFESSOR BRUCE MEYER, 2004

NOTE TO *ROSICRUCIAN IN THE BASEMENT* AND *HEAVENLY SEX*

For my podiatrist father, Rosicrucianism is allied with *Kabbalah*—Jewish mysticism—and he began, following my mother's death in 1948, to put himself "on the right track for union with the Higher Self" (his words). A small businessman practicing in a conservative Chicago neighborhood he began thinking and talking like the New Age hippies, yogis and writers I became familiar with a decade or two later.

In section 4 ("Lenore Gets On Top") of "Lenore And The Leopard Dog," unable to recall my father's exact words, I found in the lines 'There is man and woman and a third thing, too, in us…' an approximation of what I felt him to be saying or trying to say. These lines are not mine. They are a borrowing from the poet Jelaluddin Rumi, translated by Coleman Barks. A credit also appears on page 28 of the book *Heavenly Sex*. I am a student of Rumi and have been deeply influenced by him.

Dad never used the word *mandala,* but, for him, the American one dollar bill included in its "pictures" much of what he thought one needed to know about the Self and how to survive in this world and find one's way to the next. In his mind, given its symbolism, the coin of our realm was designed by Rosicrucians (or Masons) like Benjamin Franklin.

With respect to "After The ByPass" and "A Man Needs A Place To Stand," I am thinking of W.B. Yeats, that "Irish Rosicrucian," as Dad put it. For Dad, Yeats was a Rosicrucian first and a poet second.

ACKNOWLEDGMENTS

Grateful acknowledgment is made to the editors of the following publications for permission to reprint many of the poems in this book:

AIRON 9 (Buenos Aires, Argentina), Alsop Review (eZine), AMBIT (London), Another Chicago Magazine (ACM #37), ANTIOCH REVIEW, APPROACH MAGAZINE, ARTS IN SOCIETY (Madison, Wisconsin), THE ACTIVIST (Oberlin College), *ARTES/LETRES DIALOGS* (Mexico City), BELOIT POETRY JOURNAL, BEST ARTICLES & STORIES, Blue Moon Review (eZine), BookPress: The Newspaper of the Literary Arts (Ithaca, NY), CARLETON MISCELLANY, CENTER (New York), CHELSEA REVIEW (New York), CHICAGO REVIEW, EPOCH (Cornell University), CONTEMPORARY VERSE II (University of Manitoba, Canada), CROSS CANADA WRITERS QUARTERLY (Toronto), Davka, Jewish Cultural Revolution (San Francisco), DENVER QUARTERLY, DESCANT, Disquieting Muses (eZine), *EL CORNO EMPLUMADO* (Mexico City), EPOCH, THE ETRUSCAN (New South Wales, Australia), *EXPOSICION EXHAUSTIVA DE LA NUEVA POESIA GALERIA* (Montevideo, Uruguay), EQUAL TIME (New York); EXTENSIONS (New York), Fiction-Online, An Internet Literary Magazine THE FIDDLE-HEAD (New Brunswick), FROM A WINDOW (Tucson), GALLEY SAIL REVIEW, GREENFIELD REVIEW (Greenfield Center, NY), HANGING LOOSE PRESS (Brooklyn, NY), HAWAII REVIEW (Honolulu), HUDSON REVIEW, THE HUMANIST, INKSTONE (Bowling Green, Ohio), THE IOWA REVIEW, KARAKI (Victoria, B.C.), KAYAK (Santa Cruz), MALAHAT REVIEW (Victoria, B.C.), THE MARTLET (Victoria, B.C.), MASSACHUSETTS REVIEW, MATRIX (London), MICHIGAN QUARTERLY REVIEW, MT. SHASTA SELECTIONS (MSS), MONTEREY BAY POETRY FESTIVAL 2003 CHAPBOOK, Mudlark, An Electronic Journal of Poetry & Poetics (eZine), Mudlark Poster #7, THE NATION, NEW MEXICO QUARTERLY, NEW ORLEANS POETRY JOURNAL, NEW WORK #1; THE NEW YORKER, THE NEW YORK TIMES, THE NORTH AMERICAN REVIEW, NORTHERN LIGHT (University of Manitoba), THE NORTHSTONE REVIEW (Minneapolis), OCTAVO, THE PARIS REVIEW, PEARL (Denmark), PENNY POEMS, PERSPECTIVE (ST. LOUIS), POETRY CHICAGO, Poetry Magazine.com (eZine), POETRY TORONTO, POETRY AUSTRALIA, POETRY NORTHWEST, PRISM INTERNATIONAL (Vancouver, B.C.), QUARTERLY REVIEW OF LITERATURE, RAMPIKE (York University), *RealPoetik* (rpoetik, eZINe), Salt Spring Island Tatler (eZine), Santa Clara Review (Santa Clara University), THE SANTA CRUZ SENTINEL, SHENANDOAH, STONE (Ithaca, New York), SIGNAL HILL BROADSIDES (Victoria, B.C.), *Shirim* (A Jewish Poetry Journal), TAMBOURINE (St. Louis), TRANSATLANTIC REVIEW (LONDON, ENGLAND),

TRI-QUARTERLY (Evanston, Illinois), TUATARA (Victoria, B.C.), UCSC STUDENT GUIDE (Santa Cruz), WAVES (Toronto), Web Del Sol (eZine), Literary Art on the World Wide Web, WEST COAST WORKS (Vancouver, B.C.), WILD DOG, X-CONNECT (CrossConnect) (eZine), ZAHIR (Portsmouth, New Hampshire).

Some of these poems have been recorded by Western Michigan University's Aural Press (1005); the Library of Congress; National Public Radio (New Letters On The Air, University of Missouri); KPFA-FM (Berkeley, CA); and Uncle Dog Audio.

CDs include *Rosicrucian in the Basement, read by the author,* Uncle Dog Audio 1001 and *Robert Sward: Poetry, Review & Interview, with Jack Foley,* Uncle Dog Audio 1002.

Anthologized work: *A Controversy Of Poets, An Anthology Of Contemporary American Poets; Body Language, A Head To Toe Anthology; The Chicago Review Anthology; The Contemporary American Poets: American Poetry Since 1940; Following the Plough, Poems on the Land; GRRR, A Collection of Poems About Bears; Heartland: Poets Of The Midwest; I Want To Be the Poet of Your Kneecaps, Poems of Quirky Romance; Inside Outer Space; New Poems Of The Space Age; Illinois Poetry; Inventions For Imaginative Thinking; QUARRY WEST #35, (University of California at Santa Cruz), Anthology, Poets &Writers of Monterey Bay; Lighthouse Point: An Anthology of Santa Cruz Writers; Midland: 25 Years Of Fiction And Poetry; New Yorker Book Of Poems; The Now Voices; Oxford Book Of Light Verse; Penguin Book of Animal Poetry; Riverside Poetry III; Silver Screen: Neue Amerikanische Lyrik; Smaller Than God, Words of Spiritual Longing; Some Haystacks Don't Even Have Any Needle; Southern California Anthology; Sports Poems; The Practical Imagination; The Space Atlas; Stories of Our Mothers & Fathers; Tesseracts: Canadian Science Fiction; The Treasure Of Our Tongue; The Voice That Is Great Within Us; To Say The Least, Canadian Poets From A To Z; and Where Is Vietnam? American Poets Respond; X-Connect (Cross Connect), Writers of the Information Age.*

See also *"Contemporary Authors, A Bio-Bibliographical Guide,* Volume 206, 2003.

R.D. Brinkmann and Peter Behrens translated some of these poems into German in a volume titled *Silver Screen, Neue Amerikanische Lyrik,* Kiepenheuer & Witsch, Koln. Others were translated into Spanish by Madela Ezcurra and Eduwardo Costa and appeared in *AIRON* 9, Buenos Aires, Argentina.

I wish to thank the Djerassi Foundation, the Edward MacDowell Association, Yaddo, the Cultural Council of Santa Cruz County, the John Simon Guggenheim Memorial Foundation, and the Canada Council for affording me an opportunity to complete this book.